# GLOBETROTTER™

## Trave

# FLORIDA

INCLUDING **WALT DISNEY WORLD**®

## LIZ BOOTH

NEW
HOLLAND

NEW
HOLLAND

★★★ Highly recommended
★★ Recommended
★ See if you can

Fifth edition published in 2007
by New Holland Publishers (UK) Ltd
London • Cape Town • Sydney • Auckland
First published in 1997
10 9 8 7 6 5 4 3 2 1
www.newhollandpublishers.co.za

Garfield House, 86 Edgware Road
London W2 2EA, United Kingdom

80 McKenzie Street
Cape Town, 8001
South Africa

Unit 1, 66 Gibbes Street
Chatswood, NSW 2067
Australia

218 Lake Road
Northcote, Auckland
New Zealand

Distributed in the USA by
The Globe Pequot Press, Connecticut

ISBN 978 1 84537 861 5

**Keep us Current**
Information in travel guides is apt to change, which is
why we regularly update our guides. We'd be grateful
to receive feedback if you've noted something we
should include in our updates. If you have new
information, please share it with us by writing to the
Publishing Manager, Globetrotter, at the office nearest
to you (addresses on this page). The most significant
contribution to each new edition will receive a free
copy of the updated guide.

**Publishing Manager:** Thea Grobbelaar
**DTP Cartographic Manager:** Genené Hart
**Editors:** Nicky Steenkamp, Melany McCallum, Tarryn Berry,
Mary Duncan, Claudia Dos Santos
**Cartographers:** Carryck Wise, Nicole Bannister, William Smuts
**Design and DTP:** Nicole Bannister, Sonya Cupido
**Picture Researcher:** Shavonne Govender
**Compiler:** Elaine Fick

Reproduction by Hirt & Carter (Pty) Ltd, Cape Town.
Printed and bound by Times Offset (M) Sdn. Bhd., Malaysia.

Although every effort has been made to ensure that
this guide is up to date and current at time of going
to print, the Publisher accepts no responsibility or
liability for any loss, injury or inconvenience incurred
by readers or travellers using this guide.

**Cover:** *Beautiful fireworks are often displayed at the
Cinderella Castle in the Magic Kingdom®.*
**Title page:** *Miami, heart of the cruise-ship industry.*

# CONTENTS

# 1
# Introducing Florida

Flanked by the Atlantic Ocean and the Gulf of Mexico, crisscrossed by rivers and streams and dotted with lakes, Florida is dominated by water. This abundance has not only shaped the landscape, but provided a perfect playground for citizens and tourists alike.

Discover urban chic, glamour and glitz in **Miami** or head to **Orlando** and the spectacular wonders of **Walt Disney World**®, seek out the vibrance of the **Keys** or the rolling white beaches out west. Indulge in the colonial history of the former regional capitals: **Pensacola** in the northwest and **St Augustine** on the east coast. Today's state capital, **Tallahassee**, lies in the centre of the northern region, nominated as a compromise between feuding east and west coast settlers. Sprawling **Jacksonville** provides a gateway for travellers heading south from the eastern seaboard of the United States, and areas like **Daytona Beach** swarm with American visitors each spring.

Those in need of quiet will welcome the sunsets and the scenery. For nature lovers there is the hushed mystery of the **Everglades** and the underwater extravaganza of the **Florida Keys**. Snorkelling and diving are encouraged particularly in the **John Pennekamp Coral Reef State Park** in the Keys, and at **Peacock Springs State Park** at Luraville where certified divers can explore some of the 28,000ft (8500m) of surveyed caves.

For families Florida is hard to beat with its choice of theme parks from Walt Disney World® to **Busch Gardens** and **Universal Studios**®, as well as many safe beaches and a wide range of family-orientated hotels and restaurants.

**Opposite:** *Sailing, one of the attractions at St Pete Beach on the West Coast.*

**Above:** *The Everglades flow hundreds of miles, creating shady swamps that shelter alligators and other wildlife.*

## THE LAND

Geologists estimate that Florida is one of the very youngest parts of the continental United States and the last land mass to have emerged from the primordial ocean. This is a low-lying region, generally less than 100ft (30m) above sea level. The highest point, at just 345ft (105m), lies in Walton County. Nowhere in Florida is more than 60 miles (100km) from a beach.

The 450,000-acre (182,112ha) **Lake Okeechobee** is the state's largest freshwater area. It feeds into the Everglade Basin, which stretches for many miles with water just a few inches deep. Strictly speaking, this is really a slow-moving river, 150 miles (240km) long and 50 miles (80km) wide. Now a protected territory, the river-cum-swamp provides a safe haven for about 300 different species of bird, some 600 kinds of fish and a number of animals, like the rare Florida panther.

To the north Florida is dominated by great **hardwood forests** and vast open tracts of beautiful beach. The **Suwannee River** flows 177 miles (283km) and is fed by more than 20 major springs before reaching the **Gulf of Mexico**. Green, rolling hills and large pine forests dominate the northwest **Panhandle**. This beautiful area, which is edged by salt marshes and expansive, sparkling-white sand beaches has been nicknamed **The Emerald Coast**.

The deep, lush tropical forests and crystal waters of the **Florida Keys** remain a haven of peace and quiet and are perfect for exciting deep-water game fishing, coral reef diving and swimming. The string of islands curves 192 miles (309km) southwest from the mainland culminating in **Loggerhead Key** in the **Dry Tortugas**, although most people consider Key West to be the end of the line, because that's where the road ends.

## Climate

Florida earns its epithet The Sunshine State with hot summers, punctuated by tropical storms and often hurricanes. This area experiences more thunderstorms than any other part of the USA, the lightning causing numerous fires. Winters are generally warmer than in much of the United States and Europe.

The state can be divided into two climatic zones – **tropical** to the south of a line from Bradenton to Vero Beach and **subtropical** to the north. Average annual summer **temperatures** are 26.9°C (80.5°F) in the northern, and 55.1°C (82.7°F) in the southern regions. These fall each winter to about 11.7°C (53°F) in the north and 20.3°C (68.5°F) in the south.

There are however notable exceptions. Winter tourists are sometimes dismayed at the sight of **frost** as far south as Miami, though this phenomenon is rare. The Keys have never experienced frost.

Summer often brings **tropical storms** and the state averages 53in (135cm) of rain a year. This varies from about 40in (100cm) in Key West to 62in (157cm) in West Palm Beach. **Hurricanes** can occur from June to November but are most likely in September. Their movements are constantly monitored and the state has an established evacuation programme. Hurricanes can hit anywhere along the coast, though the worst is usually over within 24 hours.

## Plant Life

Florida's sandy loam and peat ground are just two of 300 local soil types, making this one of the most fertile areas in America. The state is home to over 300 tree species and more than 3500

**HURRICANES**

Florida lies in the hurricane belt and the old warning is:
June – too soon
July – stand by
August – look out you must
September – remember
October – all over
**Hurricane Andrew** was the most devastating of the recent hurricanes to hit this region. The storm devastated the Bahamas and reached southern Florida on 24 August 1992. It left 38 people dead and some 175,000 homeless.

**Below:** *Miles of white sand beaches, like Bahia Honda, line Florida's coast.*

| COMPARATIVE CLIMATE CHART | MIAMI | | | | ORLANDO | | | | PENSACOLA | | | |
|---|---|---|---|---|---|---|---|---|---|---|---|---|
| | WIN | SPR | SUM | AUT | WIN | SPR | SUM | AUT | WIN | SPR | SUM | AUT |
| | JAN | APR | JULY | OCT | JAN | APR | JULY | OCT | JAN | APR | JULY | OCT |
| AVERAGE TEMP. °C | 15 | 20 | 24 | 22 | 8 | 17 | 23 | 19 | 12 | 20 | 27 | 21 |
| AVERAGE TEMP. °F | 67 | 75 | 82 | 79 | 49 | 63 | 75 | 67 | 53 | 67 | 81 | 70 |
| HOURS OF SUN | 12 | 13 | 14 | 12 | 12 | 13 | 14 | 12 | 12 | 13 | 14 | 12 |
| RAINFALL mm | 51 | 76 | 152 | 179 | 53 | 55 | 197 | 71 | 109 | 109 | 177 | 99 |
| RAINFALL in | 2 | 3 | 6 | 7 | 2 | 2 | 8 | 3 | 4.5 | 4.5 | 7 | 4 |
| DAYS OF RAINFALL | 7 | 8 | 12 | 13 | 7 | 7 | 14 | 9 | 9 | 9 | 12 | 9 |

## MANGROVE FORESTS

Florida is home to the red, white, black and buttonwood mangroves.

**Red mangroves:** found nearest the ocean, they survive by supporting themselves on prop roots that arch deep into the ground. They provide vital nursery grounds for young reptiles, fish and birds.

**White mangroves:** prefer higher ground and grow further inland, often forming hummocks with larger land-based trees such as mahogany and gumbo-limbo.

**Black mangroves:** identified by the short, finger-like roots that are used as airways and burst out of the ground all around the tree.

**Buttonwood mangroves:** are very similar to the white mangroves, also preferring higher ground.

other plants. **Mangrove, cypress, palm, pine** and **oak** are predominant. Species like **maple** and **magnolia** are found mainly in the north.

Vast **grasslands** are found across the state, forming large, lush prairies. A unique **scrubland** covers much of the dry, sandy coasts. The freshwater and coastal **swamps** abound with trees, grasses and flowers, which provide a rich breeding ground for wildlife.

Florida is home to three diverse national forests: **Apalachicola** (hardwood/pine as well as carnivorous plants), **Osceola** (cypress swamps) and **Ocala** (desert scrub), which combined cover more than 1,000,000 acres (404,695ha) yet would all fit inside the sweeping expanse of the **Everglades National Park**. The state also offers some unusual marine parks, including the 175,000-acre (70,821ha) **Biscayne National Park** southeast of Miami which is renowned for its many shipwrecks (some dating back to the pirate days of the 16th century) the **John Pennekamp Coral Reef State Park** around Key Largo which offers divers a close-up view of living reefs, and the wildlife sanctuary **Dry Tortugas**, west of Key West. In total the state maintains some 156 parks.

Only some 40% of the land is used for agriculture, with one-third of that set aside for timber or pasture. The farmland, however, is very productive and Florida is known for its **citrus groves**, which produce about three-quarters of all the fruit sold in the entire United States.

### Wildlife

While probably most famous for its 'gators', Florida also has more than 400 types of **bird**, some 100 different species of mammal, and over 700 varieties of fish. **Panthers**, sadly, are on the endangered list, which also includes puma, boar and black bears; but rehabilitation programmes

underway at national parks throughout the state are proving successful in halting the decline of Florida's interesting fauna.

Out at sea there is a variety of dolphins and porpoises as well as the **manatee**, or sea cow. Manatees, once hunted to the brink of extinction for their meat, hide and oil, are now the object of a dedicated protection programme. There are more fish types here than anywhere else in the world, from grouper, snapper and flounder to tarpon, marlin and shark. Fishing is permitted in 35 of the Florida State Parks (www.floridastateparks.org)

Swimming in the Everglades is not recommended due to a large population of deceptively docile **alligators**. Many golf courses sport alligator warning signs at their water hazards.

Florida's climate is also enjoyed by some 40 species of snake, including venomous varieties such as two kinds of **rattlesnake** and the **copperhead**. The **coral snake** and the water- or **cottonmouth moccasin** are potentially lethal, but you are more likely to encounter them behind glass in wildlife parks than outdoors.

The coastal areas often form breeding sites for thousands of seabirds. **Bald eagles** and **turkeys** can sometimes be spotted inland and Florida houses the largest breeding colonies of egrets, herons, ibises and pelicans north of the Caribbean. In the Everglades you may be lucky enough to spot the rare **purple gallinule**.

## HISTORY IN BRIEF
### Native Americans

The earliest inhabitants, native Americans travelling from the north, discovered balmy Florida about 12,000 years ago. Awaiting them was a land of plenty teeming with wildlife and fish. Little evidence has been found to suggest that they were more than **hunter-gatherers**.

**Above:** *Manatees were thought to be mermaids by the sailors of earlier centuries.*
**Opposite:** *Florida's citrus fruit is the agricultural mainstay of the region.*
**Below:** *The beautiful and rare purple gallinule.*

**TRAIL ETIQUETTE**

- Carry away all your rubbish.
- Don't feed the animals!
- Stay on designated trails.
- Extinguish all camp fires (where permitted) after use.
- Don't bring pets into parks.
- Beware of hunting seasons.
- Avoid shining torches at nesting turtles.

Primitive irrigation ditches indicate that some of the first
farming communities existed around 500BC. Unfortunately,
many of the priceless ancient burial mounds and artefacts
have been destroyed in the continuous quest for modern
housing and development.

**European Settlers**

Florida first appears on a crude Spanish map of 1502 and a
few years later was described as the 'Land of Eternal Youth'
by European explorers. But it was Spaniard **Juan Ponce de
León** who really discovered Florida for the Europeans in
1513. Travelling north from the established Puerto Rico, he
was searching for the mythical **Fountain of Youth**. Juan
Ponce de León waded ashore on the northeast coast,
somewhere near today's St Augustine, and named the land
**'La Florida'** in honour of the Spanish Easter Festival of
Flowers, *Pascua Florida,* that had just been celebrated
aboard his ship.

Believing Florida to be no more than an island in the
Bahamas, it was a further eight years before he returned
to establish a colony in the Fort Myers area. But he and
his men were then savagely attacked by hostile Calusa
Indians. The opinion today is that the Calusas had been

forewarned by their island cousins from Puerto Rico and Haiti, who had been subjected to hardship and slavery by the Spanish overlords. De León was wounded and fled back to Cuba where he then passed away.

The next European foray into the region occurred seven years later in 1528. Lured by tales of untold treasure, another Spaniard, **Panfilo de Narváez**, landed at Tampa Bay with more than 400 men. His plan was to discover how Florida connected to Mexico, but the expedition took its toll and a further eight years went by before just four of the original party managed to find their way there.

In 1559 **Tristan de Luna y Arellano** founded a colony in Pensacola Bay with 1400 pioneers; it failed two years later when the settlement was destroyed by a hurricane. However, it was revived 139 years later and on the strength of this argument the people of today's Pensacola claim to live in Florida's oldest town – hotly disputed by the residents of St Augustine where a colony was established in 1565 by **Pedro Menéndez de Avilés**. He used this new town as a base from which to attack Fort Caroline, which had been set up by the French Huguenots and was seen as a threat to Spanish shipping lanes.

**Above:** *Pedro Menéndez de Avilés was one of the first Europeans to set foot in Florida.*
**Opposite:** *Calusa Indians at the time of arrival of the European explorers.*
**Below:** *This lovely 12th-century monastery was transported from Spain and reconstructed in Florida.*

## Spanish Dominance

The Spanish retained control of Florida for almost two centuries despite constant warring with local Indians, the French from the Louisiana area and the British living in Carolina and Georgia. Towns were often under siege, and St Augustine endured a 52-day attack on one occasion. Even **Sir Francis Drake** made his bid for Florida with a failed attack in 1586.

## HISTORICAL CALENDAR

**1497** Europeans see Florida for the first time and record it on maps.

**1513** Juan Ponce de León wades ashore and names the land 'La Florida' after the Spanish Festival of Flowers.

**1559** Tristan de Luna lands and settles at Pensacola, but is forced to withdraw two years later after a devastating hurricane.

**1565** Pedro Menéndez de Avilés founds the first settlement at St Augustine for Spanish King Philip II.

**1763** After a century of raids by native Americans, French and British, the Spanish relinquish Florida to England in exchange for Havana, Cuba.

**1783** British cede Florida back to the Spanish.

**1785** The start of three years' skirmishing between Spanish

and American forces.

**1813–18** General Andrew Jackson enters western Florida to campaign against native Americans in three wars.

**17 July 1821** General Jackson receives Florida for the United States from the Spanish in a ceremony in Pensacola.

**1822** A Florida government is established under Governor William Duval.

**1836** The St Joseph to Lake Wimico rail track is the very first line to operate in the state of Florida.

**1842** The Second Seminole War ends with the transfer of nearly 4000 Seminole Indians to Arkansas and Oklahoma.

**1845** Florida officially becomes the 27th state of the United States with William D Moseley as governor.

**1855–58** The third and

final Seminole Indian war takes place.

**1894** Henry Flagler completes railroad as far as Palm Beach.

**1958** National Aeronautics and Space Administration (NASA), starts work at Cape Canaveral.

**16 July 1969** The historic Apollo 11 mission lifts off from Cape Kennedy to carry the first men to the moon.

**1 October 1971** Walt Disney World® opens the Magic Kingdom® in Orlando.

**1981** The first manned space shuttle is launched from John F Kennedy Space Center.

**2000** By the turn of the new century, Florida's population had grown to almost 16 million, making it the fourth most populous in the US.

In 1763 British forces gained control of Florida in a swap for Havana, Cuba, as part of the **Treaty of Paris**, the final settlement of the Seven Year War which had devastated Europe. This ended military rule, with the army exchanged for civil servants. However, Florida did not remain British for long. It

was used as a base against the colonists in the **American War of Independence**. After losing their battle, the British handed Florida back to Spain in return for the Bahamas.

## United States Control and the Seminole Wars

The new Americans and the Spanish Floridians constantly battled over the border.

**General Andrew Jackson** from Tennessee finally swayed the balance by capturing Pensacola which led to Spain's cession of Florida to the United States on 17 July 1821.

By this time the various native American tribes were collectively known as the **Seminoles**, from *se-mi-no-lee* (a Creek word meaning 'runaway'). The

reluctant Indians were hustled out of their territories and despatched unceremoniously; many fled and sought refuge in the forests and swamps, hence their name. The **First Seminole War** took place during 1817–18. A second war followed between 1835–42, culminating in the Removal Act which resulted in most of the Seminole Indians being sent off to Arkansas and Oklahoma.

**Tallahassee**, originally a native American village, was made the territory capital in 1824 to end arguments between Pensacola and St Augustine over which had the right to lead the region. Indians were not the only problem facing the settlers. St Joseph was a boom town in 1835, competing with nearby Apalachicola as a trading port. But the flourishing community of some 12,000 people vanished within nine years, the result of a deadly outbreak of yellow fever and a destructive hurricane.

During the epidemic Apalachicola fared better, with some help from bank director and postmaster **John Gorrie** who was also a doctor. He treated his yellow fever sufferers by cooling their rooms. John Gorrie did not live to see the eventual fruits of his research. Ridiculed in New York, he died a broken man survived by his invention: the forerunner of the fridge and of the air conditioner.

Florida became an American state in 1845 by which time only a few hundred Seminoles were left. A third and final war, sparked off by an unfortunate misunderstanding, erupted between 1855–58, leading to great loss of life

**Above:** *Floridians are proud of their history and love to re-enact the past. Here a man is dressed like a 17th-century soldier at Castillo de San Marcos.*
**Opposite:** *Castillo de San Marcos, a 17th-century Spanish castle and now one of the top attractions in St Augustine.*

**Right:** *Florida's citrus fruit is exported all over the world.*
**Opposite:** *Railroad king, Henry M Flagler, brought the first railway lines down to Miami and transformed the region.*

before the proud native Americans finally had to concede defeat. A small number still live in the Everglades.

## Civil War

The battles of the **American Civil War** largely passed Florida by. A total of 1290 men joined the Union Army (the Yankee North) which captured several of Florida's seaports. Pensacola was one such city with the **Yankees** holding Fort Pickens and the **Confederacy** in control of Fort McRee. The southern rebels were the first to crack, fleeing the city in 1862. Fort Pickens escaped civil war skirmishes and became the area's first tourist attraction when the government imprisoned **Chief Geronimo** here in 1886. Crowds used to gather outside to see the Apache Indian in captivity.

## Railroad

The Tallahassee to St Marks railroad, conceived and financed by wealthy entrepreneurs from northern Florida who gradually opened up the southern end of the state – helped by the enthusiasm of existing residents – operated from 1837–84. Miami was first developed in the 1860s and 1870s but it was not until 1894, when local resident **Julia Tuttle** sent a fresh orange blossom north to railroad magnate **Henry M Flagler** in frosty Palm Beach to persuade him to bring the track all the way south, that things really started to happen.

### PLIGHT OF THE NATIVE AMERICAN

The arrival of Europeans in the 1500s forced the native Americans to fight for every inch of their ancestral land. By 1800, only a handful of the once proud **Tequesta** and **Calusa** Indian population remained alive.

At this time, **Creek** and **Muskogee** tribes, known collectively as Seminoles, were forced south by the encroaching development of the United States of America. They settled in Florida, raiding settlements and providing shelter for runaway slaves. Three wars followed, during which most Seminoles were killed or forcibly removed to reservations in Alabama and Oklahoma. Only about 150 hid deep in the swamps, forming the basis of the small community left today.

Henry Flagler extended the Florida East Coast Railway down through the Florida Keys in 1912. Although the track was destroyed by the hurricane of 1935, the same path was followed during construction of the existing Overseas Highway.

The start of the tourist trade and the expansion of agriculture both date back to the railroad development of the late 1800s. Now, for the first time farmers could export their goods nationwide and visitors could take advantage of Florida's warm winters.

## Booming Miami

The original 'jetsetters' discovered Miami and the wonderful south early in the 20th century and a property boom followed. Devastating hurricanes in 1926 and 1935 failed to stop the flow of money into the fledgling city and various events shaped and moulded its ambience. The famous Art Deco area of Miami was developed in 1930, while the 1960s saw the arrival of **Cubans** fleeing the revolutionary Fidel Castro.

Most of the Cuban refugees lived in temporary ghettos, but the failure of the 'Bay of Pigs' invasion of 1961 and the threatening Cuban Missile Crisis of 1962 convinced the growing exile community that it would be a long time before they could return home. With time they came to lend a strong new Latin-American flavour to Miami.

## Modern-day Florida

Further north the government was investing in outer space and the National Aeronautics and Space Administration (**NASA**) began operations at Cape Canaveral. The historic Apollo 11 mission was launched here on 16 July 1969, taking the first men to the moon. Twelve years later the first space shuttle lifted off from the **John F Kennedy Space Center**.

### THE CIVIL WAR YEARS

When Florida was at its peak as a plantation state some 39,000 out of a population of about 87,000 were slaves. The third state to join the pro-slavery **Confederate** cause, Florida seceded from the **Union** (the northern states) in 1861. It supplied food and arms to the cause as well as thousands of men – only 1290 of them joined the Union army. Although Union soldiers occupied most of the seaports to mount a blockade against the Confederacy, the state really only suffered two battles. In February 1864 the **Battle of Olustee**, near Live Oak, cost 300 lives with both sides claiming victory. The more decisive victory came at Tallahassee a year later when a group of raw recruits saved the capital from falling into the hands of the Union.

**Below:** *A space shuttle blasts off from the John F Kennedy Space Center.*

The state has continued to develop rapidly and although recession has slowed the property boom, thousands of older people still make Florida their retirement home and plenty of others are still immigrating to the state; jointly, tourism and agriculture remain its most valuable industries. By 2005 the population of Florida had grown to an estimated 17,789,864, making it the fourth most populated state in the United States after California, New York and Texas. The population grew more than 11% between 2000 and 2005, double the speed of the United States as a whole.

## GOVERNMENT AND ECONOMY

The state government was formally established in 1885, although it has been modified frequently since then. The most recent changes occurred in 1968 when the electorate approved 20 revisions to the constitution.

Florida is ruled by a **governor** and **lieutenant governor** (these two candidates run as a team during elections), as well as six **cabinet members** – a secretary of state, attorney general, treasurer, comptroller and commissioners of education and agriculture. The Executive is supported by a **Senate** of 40 and the **House of Representatives** with 120 members.

### Economic Development

Throughout the 1800s Florida's rapid economic development mirrored the expansion of the railroad system. Until 1821 the entire region was little more than an unexploited backwater, then the railroad magnates began to look further south, thereby prompting industrial growth.

The original industries, **agriculture** and **tourism**, still dominate. Even today, enduring development and success depends heavily on a reliable transport network. Railroads continue to play an

important part, though air travel has improved east-west links like those from Miami to Tampa.

Miami International Airport is a major hub for the region, serving not only Europe but the Caribbean and Latin America, while Orlando is developing its international links, particularly in the charter market.

Roads play an even greater role and a network of highways links most of the major centres. The **Overseas Highway** is the main access route into the Florida Keys for most tourist traffic.

With so much coastline, **shipping** is vital and the state boasts eight deep-water ports and more than 994 miles (1600km) of navigable waterways.

## Tourism and Agriculture

Tourism is the state's largest industry and, despite a dip in the early 1990s, has been growing steadily for the past decade. Tourism grew nearly 5% in 2005 to a record 83.6 million, after a 7% increase in 2004. In 2002, the state attracted 73.9 million visitors but numbers were down in 2006 in reaction to the high number of hurricanes hitting the state in 2005.

Florida provides the United States with 75% of its **citrus fruit** and is second only to California in vegetable production, with **tomatoes** the leading crop. The state also provides about 40% of the nation's **sugar cane**, as well as greenhouse and foliage plants. **Timber** is harvested in the north while the southern and central grasslands sustain the state's livestock and thoroughbred racehorses.

**TIME TO CHANGE**

Florida has two time zones – Eastern Standard and Central Standard Time. The state is located in the south rather than the east but such was the power of the railroad magnates, that it was included in Eastern Standard Time in order to make the rail timetables more convenient.

Eastern Standard Time is five hours behind Greenwich Mean Time, while the area to the west of the Apalachicola River is on Central Standard Time, six hours behind GMT. The United States has instituted Daylight Saving in the summer, bringing clocks forward by one hour.

**Below:** *Florida is governed from the Senate House in Tallahassee.*

*Above: A native American guide navigates an airboat tour through the Everglades.*

## THE PEOPLE

Despite a comparatively slow start, Florida's population boomed during the 20th century and is today the fourth largest in the United States with some 17.8 million residents. People are concentrated mainly in the **urban belts** with vast areas of the state relatively untouched.

Floridians represent a rich cultural mix of racial and ethnic groups, each lending their special character, colour and spirit. The official language is English, though in some sections of Miami Spanish prevails. Place names have been influenced by both the original native American inhabitants and the Spanish.

### Native Americans

The arrival of Europeans during the 16th century left the native American population decimated by disease, slavers, land disputes and wars. By the time the United States gained control, only some 5000 **Seminoles** remained. Many were relocated to Arkansas and Oklahoma; a final 150 fled deep into the Everglades, eking out an existence with fishing and hunting.

The past few years have seen a change in attitude towards native Americans, who at last have been accorded the deserved respect. Today the descendants of the original native Americans live in three **reservations** in southern Florida (Big Cypress, Miccosukee and Seminole Indian Reserve); here they use their knowledge of the Glades as a way to earn money. You can take a trip into the swamps accompanied by a Seminole guide and experience a fascinating glimpse of Indian life in one of the nearby villages.

They are a proud people coming to terms with past injustices, poverty and hardship, in an effort to reclaim their rightful place in modern Florida without losing touch with their ancient heritage and customs.

## The African-Americans

After the United States won control of Florida in1821, white planters began to develop massive plantations, relying on slave labour. Large numbers of Africans were forcibly shipped in to man

these new plantations and citrus groves, and by the 1830s the white and black communities were of approximately equal size, numbering some 11,000 each. Although sparsely populated southern parts of Florida offered refuge for runaway slaves, northern Florida remained for a long time the deepest of the Deep South, both socially and politically. Slavery was, in principle, ended by the Civil War, but the agricultural patterns of Florida stayed ingrained for another fifty years.

Eventually the arrival of tourism offered opportunities for African-Americans, though it was not until the 1964 Civil Rights Act that wider based civil liberty could be guaranteed. Today, African-Americans form a smaller proportion of the population, outnumbered by the influx of white migrants that has taken place since the 1900s.

## Senior Citizens

Florida's demographic statistics changed dramatically with the arrival of the 'blue-rinse brigade' in the early 20th century. Numbers of white residents climbed rapidly as retirees from the northern states recognized that Florida winters were much kinder on old bones. Now every year thousands of senior citizens choose to retire in the sun. Although retirees came to dominate Miami Beach, in particular, from the 1970s, many new arrivals opt for Florida's small rural towns thereby contributing to a drop in the average age of beach city residents.

**Above:** *Tourists flock to admire the view from Sunset Pier, Key West.*

### PUBLIC HOLIDAYS

**1 January** • New Year's Day
**15 January** •
Martin Luther King's Birthday
**3rd Monday in February** •
Presidents Day
**Last Monday in May** •
Memorial Day
**4 July** • Independence Day
**1st Monday in September** •
Labor Day
**2nd Monday in October** •
Columbus Day
**11 November** •
Veteran's Day
**Last Thursday in November** •
Thanksgiving Day
**25 December** •
Christmas Day
Americans generally have less holiday than Europeans, with only a day off at Christmas and Easter. October 31 (**Halloween**) is almost a holiday, with kids 'trick or treating', nowadays usually by car for safety.

## TOURISM

More than 83.6 million tourists visited Florida in 2005. Numbers fell in 2006 because of the bad hurricanes in 2005 but officials are confident numbers will start climbing again. More than 80% of all visitors come from other parts of the United States, some 2.5 million from Canada and a further 1.2 million from the UK. Tourism directly employs 870,100 Floridians, and in 2000 generated US$50.8 billion for the state. In 2001 almost 12 million passengers travelled through Florida's ports – led by Port of Canaveral with 3.5 million passengers making it the busiest cruise terminal in the world.

## The Cubans

Although the Fidel Castro-led 1959 **revolution in Cuba** was initially popular, many Cubans became disillusioned. Between 1965 and 1973, 230,000 arrived in Miami on the so-called 'freedom fights' from Havana, joining the 50,000 or so Cubans already in the city. Most settled along SW Eighth Street, soon better-known by its Spanish name, Calle Ocho, forming the core of what became **Little Havana**. Steady upward mobility has seen Cuban-Americans become highly influential in Miami life, and in shaping US-Cuban relations.

Most Cubans in Florida still live in and around the Miami area, contributing to the tangible Spanish feel of a city where English often seems to be a second language. Yet the community of Dade County successfully vetoed a move to have Miami declared officially bilingual. At **carnival** time, Calle Ocho in Little Havana comes alive to the throbbing sounds of Cuban music, the fragrant smell of Cuban cigars and the exuberant, vivid colours of the costumes.

## Art and Culture

Although the state of Florida is little over 170 years old it has a remarkable diversity of art and culture. Much of its history is on display and a willingness to preserve the past has ensured that attractions are easily accessible to visitors.

**Below:** *Cubans started arriving in large numbers in Florida in the 1960s.*

**Sarasota** has become the nerve centre of Florida's traditional arts. This central western town was home to the flamboyant circus master **John Ringling**, who lovingly built a 30-room Venetian-style mansion as a gift for his wife before splashing out another fortune on the **John and Mable Ringling Museum of Art**, which now contains the world's finest collection of works by Flemish artist Rubens, and again on the **Circus Museum**, filled with memorabilia from The Greatest Show on Earth. Don't miss the state's only 18th-century Italian theatre, the **Asolo Theater,** and its Center for the Performing Arts, dismantled in Italy, and shipped and reassembled in Florida in the 1950s.

**Left:** *Florida prides itself on its arts and culture. The Kravis Cultural Center in West Palm Beach is one of the leading venues.*

Nearby **Tampa** has one of only four museums in the country dedicated exclusively to African-American Art. Also in Tampa is an interesting Museum of Art with seven galleries of Greek and Roman antiquities, plus the **Tampa Bay Performing Arts Center**. Elsewhere be sure to visit the Underwater Demolition Team **SEAL** (Sea, Air and Land) **Museum** in Fort Pierce, which was a training site for navy divers in 1943, and the **American Police Hall of Fame** and Museum in Miami.

For historical interest the spotlight has to fall on **Pensacola** and **St Augustine**, the two cities vying for the right to the title 'Oldest in Florida'. Visit Seville, Palafox and the North Hill Preservation District of Pensacola or see The Old Jail, The Oldest House, the Oldest Store Museum and the Oldest Wooden Schoolhouse, all in St Augustine, which also offers a restored Spanish Quarter complete with costumed guides and a daily re-enactment of life 400 years ago. On the third Saturday night in June each year a torch-lit procession winds its way through St Augustine's old quarter, part of a Spanish Night Watch festival.

Though Florida escaped most of the horrors of the Civil War, some events are remembered annually, such as the **Battle of Natural Bridge** at which the Confederacy managed to save Tallahassee from falling into the hands of the Union forces. Each February some 2000 volunteers in full uniform relive the battle at **Lake City**. A month later the soldiers are out in force again some 62 miles (100km) to the west, to commemorate the **Battle of Olustee**.

## FESTIVALS

People in Florida need little excuse to party, but here are some of the main annual events:

**December–January** • Orange Bowl Festival, Miami.
**6 January** • Greek Orthodox Epiphany, Tarpon Springs.
**January** • Art Deco Weekend, Miami Beach.
**February** • Florida Citrus Festival and Polk County Fair, Winter Haven.
**February** • Gasparilla Festival, celebrates the pirate's invasion of Tampa, with music and street parades.
**February** • Speed Weeks and Daytona 500, Daytona.
**March** • Florida Strawberry Festival, Plant City.
**March** • Carnaval Miami, Latin American/Cuban celebrations staged by the Little Havana Tourist Authority.
**Mid-March and early July** • All-Florida Championship Rodeo, Arcadia.
**June** • Fiesta of Five Flags, Pensacola, celebration and re-enactment of De Luna's landing in 1559.
**July** • Hemingway Days Festival, Key West, includes plays, literary competition and a look-alike contest.
**October** • Destin Seafood Festival.

**Above:** *A mural in Ybor City, the Cuban heartland on the West Coast.*

Of Florida's countless festivals the **Art Deco Weekend Festival** in Miami Beach and the **Hemingway Festival** on Key West are probably the best known. **Carnaval Miami**, held each March, is an introduction to the Hispanic culture of the city.

### Sports

In the Sunshine State the emphasis is on outdoor life with a dazzling array of sports facilities and outdoor activities. Camping in national parks, barbecuing in the backyard and volleyball on the beach have become an integral part of Florida's culture.

Traditional American sports such as **baseball** and **American football** are well represented and you'll stumble into **basketball** and **volleyball** nets and goals on almost every beach and in many parks.

**Tennis** facilities still manage to outnumber golf courses, with more than 7700 around the state. These vary from a court alongside a hotel or park to upmarket Key Biscayne in Miami with its championship courts.

**National football league** teams include the Miami Dolphins, the Tampa Bay Buccaneers and the Jacksonville Jaguars. The **National Basketball Association** is represented by the Miami Heat and Orlando Magic teams while the

#### JAI ALAI

Introduced into Miami by the Cubans, this game originated in the **Basque** region of Spain. It is played in a 176ft (53m) walled court called a *fronton*. The players (*pelotaris*), wearing basket-like gloves called *cestas*, hurtle balls (*pelotas*) around the court at lightning speeds of up to 170mph (275kph) while spectators bet on the winning order. Courts exist in Fort Lauderdale, West Palm Beach, Orlando, Ocala and Daytona Beach. But the oldest *fronton*, built in 1926, is in Miami, where matches are played daily.

**Major league baseball** teams include the Florida Marlins. **National hockey league** teams are the Florida Panthers and Tampa Bay Lightning.

**Motor-sport** enthusiasts should head for Daytona or Sebring for the Daytona 500 and endurance racing. **Horse racing** takes place in Gulfstream Park and the Pompano Harness Track offers trotting races, including the Breeders' Crown with its US$1 million prize money.

**Above:** *Yacht Race Week off Key West attracts hundreds of participants.*

### Fishing and Water Sports

Water sports are split between fresh and salt, in and on! **Fishermen** have the choice of more than 7700 lakes, covering a total of 10 acres, as well as 1350 miles (2173km) of coastline. Deep-sea and big game fishing is an exciting option and day charters are widely available.

For water lovers there is the choice between surfing at Daytona Beach, snorkelling off the Florida Keys or scuba diving in natural caves. **Sailing**, **windsurfing** and **water-skiing** are offered around the coast as well as on the larger lakes, while **canoeing** has become a popular holiday in its own right as visitors explore the waterways, especially in winter when there are no tropical storms and the mosquito plague is not so intense. Greater Fort Lauderdale claims to be the **yachting** capital of the world with more than 42,000 vessels registered locally.

Swimmers have an overwhelming range of stunning beaches to choose from, as well as lakes and rivers. Note that **swimming** is not recommended in the Everglades where you may suddenly be joined by a devoted 'gator. Most of the beaches have lifeguards to advise on safety or changing weather conditions. Fort Lauderdale has the **International Swimming Hall of Fame**, complete with training facilities for swimmers and divers.

BASEBALL

Florida's major league baseball teams are the **Tampa Bay Devil Rays**, based in St Petersburg and the **Florida Marlins**. Each year hosts the Grapefruit League when 20 of the 28 major league teams travel to Florida for warmer weather and the start of spring training. Baseball league championships take place between April and September. Supreme importance is attached to the World Series, a play-off between the two best-placed teams which is held each October.

**Above:** *Palm Beach Golf Course is one of the 1100 courses across the state.*

## Golf

Florida boasts around 10% of the golf courses in the United States. Tournaments take place throughout the year and a number of courses can be booked via tour operators before you depart from your home country.

Many courses form part of luxury resorts. But be warned, an additional hazard in Florida are the alligators – heed the warning signs – which really do live in the waterways of some of the golf courses!

## Attractions

Florida could rightly claim to be the playground of the world, containing literally hundreds of theme parks and attractions. The range is broad, from quaint, old-world museums to technological marvels. Every city has its theme parks and tourist attractions but central Florida is probably the heart of the industry.

The theme park industry is so prized that the state has its own **Florida Attraction Association** providing information on the top venues. Each attraction is constantly upgraded and millions of dollars are spent on sensational new rides.

Young and old want to meet Mickey Mouse at the massive **Walt Disney World® Resort**. The Disney Resort not only includes such delights as the Magic Kingdom® and Epcot®, but also Disney-Animal Kingdom®, some fine hotels and five championship golf courses for tired dads.

The Attraction Association has a total of no less than 26 parks listed in central Florida, from **Adventure Island** and the lovely zoo at **Busch Gardens** in Tampa Bay to **Gatorland**. Parks range from historical **Medieval Times** to the excitement of **Wet 'n Wild®**.

If you are a fan of outer space visit the fascinating **Kennedy Space Center Spaceport USA** where you'll be thrilled by movies of shuttle take-offs and landings and may even be lucky enough to witness a shuttle blasting

### WALT DISNEY WORLD®

- Employs more than 55,000 cast members during busy periods, making it the largest single-site employer in the US.
- Has a daily population of 200,000 people.
- More than 2600 couples get married here every year
- The 47-sq-mile (111km²) area cost Walt Disney US$6 million.
- Opened in 1971 and was the first theme park in the Orlando area
- Employs 650 full-time gardeners who plant three million new bedding plants every year and mow 2000 lawns and fairways three times a week.
- Has more than 800 hanging baskets in constant bloom.

into orbit. This is backed up by the **US Astronaut Hall of Fame** where visitors can try the full-scale orbiter mock-up, whirling centrifuge and flight simulators.

South Florida attractions are more water-orientated. The **Billie Swamp Safari** features Seminole Indian shows and tours through the swamps, **Fury Catamarans** sail daily to the reef around the Keys and the **Jungle Queen** claims 50 years of serving the best shrimp-barbecue dinners while cruising out of Miami.

The more mechanically-minded will be interested in the **Henry Morrison Flagler Museum** in Miami, which pays tribute to the admirable railroad magnate. There's also the **Miami Museum of Science and Space Transit Planetarium**, as well as the **Weeks Air Museum** which hosts spectacular air shows.

Northern Florida's attractions tend to be more historical in flavour: displays of quaint Victorian bric-a-brac and train rides through the fine old streets of St Augustine. Pensacola is home to the **National Museum of Naval Aviation** and St Augustine has the eerie **Potter's Wax Museum** where more than 170 figures are represented.

## Shopping

An attraction in its own right, shopping in Florida is a must for any visitor. With prices approximately a third lower than

*Above: The spectacular water-ski display at SeaWorld®, Orlando, is a favourite with spectators.*

### WHEN TO GO

There are definitely 'in' seasons when the majority of parks are extremely crowded and there are long queues for every ride. December to February offers the best climate with lower temperatures and less chance of rain, although you must be prepared for cool evenings. Late August until just before Christmas is normally quiet. Crowds turn up at Christmas, Easter and on major holiday weekends. Europeans arrive in droves from mid-June to mid-August when the weather warms up, with average temperatures around 30°C (90°F) and afternoon thunderstorms.

**Above:** *Shopping is not limited to factory outlets – kiosks are equally popular.*

in Europe, and huge ranges of stock, it's very difficult indeed to resist the gigantic shopping malls that cater for the masses.

Even those with just a few hours in transit at Miami International Airport can catch a cab (taxi) to one of the nearby shopping malls to pick up a few bargains. **Westland Mall, Bayside Marketplace, Dadeland Mall** and the **Falls Shopping Center** are all within easy reach of the airport and offer a stunning variety of goods.

Shopping assumes entertainment proportions at places like the **Fort Lauderdale Swap Shop** which lures young and old with fairground rides and circus performances, and **Old Town** in Kissimmee which has an antique carousel and Ferris wheel.

Speciality shops abound, but outlet malls such as the gigantic **Sawgrass Mills Mall** outside Fort Lauderdale have become big business in the past few years, offering clothing at less-than-retail prices.

### Food and Drink

The great attraction of eating out in Florida is the variety on offer and the cost. If you fancy a 'chilli dog' for breakfast, someone will be selling one. Equally, if you want a complete meal for less than US$15 it will be available somewhere.

Ethnic restaurants mingle with American diners, fast-food outlets and seafood eateries. As well as ensuring a delectable smorgasbord of **seafood**, Florida's extensive coastline has led to the establishment of numerous immigrant pockets in the

---

**FOOD FOR THOUGHT**

The tasty cuisine of the Keys includes such local delicacies as **stone crabs**; **bollos**, a form of hush puppy; **lechon**, a roast pork dish, flavoured with oranges and garlic; **conch**, shellfish cooked into chowder (soup) using secret recipes or mixed raw with lemon juice to form conch cevice and served as a starter; and of course **Key lime pie**, much copied, but never quite the same without the juice and rind of the Key limes that are grown only here.

## CITRUS FRUITS

Polk County lies at the heart of the citrus belt thanks to its warm, sunny winters and hot summers. Lemon, lime and grapefruit are among the top crops but oranges are king, helping the state earn US$1.2 billion from its fruit annually. The first orange was thought to have been imported by the Spanish and now Florida exports a quarter of the world's orange crop. The only real threat to crops is the weather – an unexpected frost can destroy the year's harvest overnight.

cities specializing in their own cuisine. Miami has gained international recognition for its good **Cuban** food. *Platanitos* (plantain chips) and *tortilla de papa* (a Spanish omelette) are just two of the mouthwatering options. **Key lime pie** (which traditionally is yellow, not green, and served chilled, not frozen) is a must on many restaurant menus, each one claiming to make the best and most authentic one – try Sloppy Joe's in Key West.

**Stone crabs** are a south Florida delicacy, served with mayonnaise or 1000-island dressing. These particular crabs are strictly protected and may only be caught at certain times of the year once they have reached an acceptable size.

Most cities have areas where many restaurants are concentrated – all you have to do is choose which gourmet delight to sample. Try Ybor City in Tampa, the Art Deco cafés of Miami or City Walk in Orlando.

Drinks complementing the meals are just as varied. American **beers** include Budweiser, Miller and Michelob, while Heineken leads the imports. You will be served iced water at every meal, though mineral water counts as an extra. Most soft drinks are available, except for tonic water – instead you'll be offered soda water, which is not as bitter. Be sure to try out the fresh **juices** – orange and grapefruit are musts – the main ingredient of many a cocktail, along with rum bought in from nearby Caribbean islands.

**Above:** *Seafood, fresh from the ocean, is on offer in the markets.*
**Below:** *This shop in John's Pass is paradise for anyone with a sweet tooth.*

# 2
# The Southeast

A hot city with a volatile Latin temperament, gleaming skyscrapers, clandestine wheeler-dealing and golden beaches packed with 'babes', is how many people picture **Miami**, capital of the Southeast.

But the *Miami Vice* image of the city is only partly accurate: it has far more to offer. The surrounding region presents a palm-dotted coastline with warm ocean waves, and the staggering **Everglades**. The Southeast is one of America's biggest playgrounds and visitors flock in their millions to frolic in the sun, swim in the lakes, dive among underwater corals, race yachts offshore, gamble, eat out, or simply sleep in.

Flying above **Miami International Airport** you can't fail to be impressed by the city's waterways. Cruise ships steam out of the harbour, powerboats lace the ocean with white spray and swift jet-skis roar between everything.

Despite being one of the last areas of the United States to be developed (the city only dates back a hundred years) Miami has become the region's focal point. Further up the coast millionaires in search of winter sun made their opulent homes in areas like **Palm Beach**, which exudes money with its polo grounds, manicured golf courses and glitzy boutiques.

Nearby **Fort Lauderdale** is a well-off, middle-class neighbourhood with a myriad channels and a bustling cruise port filled with yachts of every size. Travelling north you reach **Martin County** where state parks and towns like **Stuart**, which dates back to the 1880s, lend a nostalgic flavour of life gone by.

### DON'T MISS

**\*\*\* South Beach**, Miami: one of the hottest places to see and be seen.
**\*\* Miami:** a downtown skyline made famous by many films, and just as spectacular in real life.
**\*\*\* Shopping:** some of the biggest malls in the world with great prices.
**\*\* Eating out:** both Miami and Fort Lauderdale pride themselves on their huge variety of venues.
**\*\*\* The Everglades:** natural wonderland threatened by encroaching development.

**Opposite:** *One of the first sights to greet tourists arriving in Miami by air.*

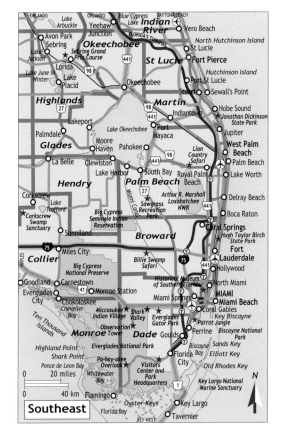

**Southeast**

## MIAMI

Miami and Miami Beach are actually two different cities, each with its own mood. Miami's mainland metropolis was little more than an overgrown village until the 1890s, when one local resident, **Julia Tuttle**, persuaded railroad king **Henry Flagler** to extend his tracks further south. By 1896 Miami was officially a city and by 1897 the first tourists arrived. But those early visionaries wanted Miami to be more than a mere **tourist resort** and so started to develop its port facilities. Today it is a major **crossroads** between United States, Caribbean and Latin America. Exploring the area as a whole is best done by car, but there are alternatives, particularly in the downtown region. Take a Metromover (individual motorized cars on a track) from **College/Bayside Station** and enjoy the skyline views. Two Metromover loops, both taking about 10 minutes, afford an excellent taste of the city atmosphere.

### Downtown **

The **Bayside Marketplace**, a short walk from the station across Biscayne Blvd, is a waterfront paradise with more than 150 speciality shops, a large marina, food halls and street entertainers. It also offers frequent free music concerts, especially jazz and reggae. Skyscrapers are filling the Miami skyline; some 45 skyscrapers taller than 152m

(500ft) are under construction or have been approved and will be built in the next five years. The tallest of them is Met 3, which should be completed by 2009 and will be 264m (866ft) tall with 75 stories. At the moment, the award goes to the Four Seasons Hotel and Tower, Miami's and Florida's tallest building, which is in use as hotel, office and residential at 240m (789ft) high and 64 stories. The Metromover takes you on to **Dade County Court-house** (Government Center Station), once the tallest building south of Washington DC. Across the street is the **Metro–Dade Cultural Center**, a complex of water features and courtyards which houses three important buildings: the **Miami–Dade Main Library**, the **Center for Fine Arts** and the **Historical Museum of Southern Florida**. The landmark **Gusman Center for the Performing Arts**, which offers numerous ballet and symphonic orchestra performances, can be found near First Street Station, on **Flagler Street**.

**Above:** *The Biltmore Hotel – a reminder of bygone glories.*

To explore the rest of Miami you need a car. **Coconut Grove**, first settled in 1884, was Miami's first real community. Today its emphasis is on the wealthy, and chic boutiques and elegant restaurants lie alongside tiny bars and street cafés. **CocoWalk** is at the heart, with retail and entertainment outlets in a European village-style setting. Be sure to visit the **Barnacle**, home of Miami pioneer Commodore Ralph Munroe, which contains much of its original furniture. **Charles Avenue**, the home of many Bahamian settlers who arrived in the late 1880s, retains its Victorian charm with red-brick sidewalks and ornate street lights. The pretty **Coconut Grove Playhouse** hosts Broadway plays each winter.

**Coral Gables**, the first planned community in the United States, was the brainchild of George Merrick. Its appeal has to do with the different 'village' designs, each

## LITTLE HAVANA

Little Havana, southwest of the downtown area, was the first stop for Cubans leaving their island after the Fidel Castro revolution, in the 1960s and 70s. Most of the original exiles have moved on, but there is still a Caribbean vibrancy to the area which is now home to a mix of Cubans, Nicaraguans and Colombians. The main street, Calle Ocho, is lined with coffee shops and fruit stalls. Try out specialities like plantain, rice and beans, chicken and pork, all cooked Cuban-style. The whole place comes alive each March for the week-long Little Havana festival, Carnaval Miami. On 17 April Cubans remember those who died in the failed Bay of Pigs invasion, with a ceremony on Cuban Memorial Boulevard.

## KEY BISCAYNE

Key Biscayne, a former coconut plantation, has remained relatively undeveloped, though affordable only to the very wealthy. It is accessible and worth a visit, as it offers one of the best beaches in Miami. **Crandon Park Beach** is rated among the top 10 in the country with its manicured grassy fringes and clean sand. **Virginia Key** to the north is site of the **Miami Seaquarium**, home of the TV star Flipper as well as Lolita, the killer whale.

representing the architectural style of a particular country or people, such as Chinese, Dutch–South African, French and Spanish. The **Biltmore Hotel**, a replica of the Giralda tower, is a classic Spanish example. Downtown Coral Gables also has its own shoppers' heaven, the **Miracle Mile**, lined with inviting shops and restaurants.

## MIAMI BEACH

Miami Beach is a seperate city to Miami and relishes its reputation as one of the hottest, hippest destinations in the United States. Singer Gloria Estefan and Island Records founder, Chris Blackwell, are among the celebrities who own hotels here. Aspirant models strive to be noticed at the top clubs and restaurants, many of which are owned by the likes of actor Sean Penn, and the popstar formerly known as Prince. You'll recognize so many settings that sometimes it may seem as as though you had wandered onto a film set by mistake.

**Miami Beach**

### Art Deco District ★★★

Miami Beach, a collection of 17 islands in **Biscayne Bay**, was first developed by millionaire promoter Carl Graham Fisher in 1912 and has enjoyed 'boom or bust' prosperity since then. The famous **Art Deco District** along Ocean Drive was the product of a boom, enjoying a massive revival in the 1990s. At the **Art Deco Welcome Center** you can obtain details of the 800 protected buildings in the area and book walking or cycling tours.

**Ocean Drive** has proved a sublime film setting: pastel-hued buildings, vibrant blue skies, swaying palm trees and the ocean beyond create a perfect backdrop. **Collins Avenue** lies a block further and is another delight of grand architecture and fading glory. The Leslie, Impala, Carlyle and Cavalier are just some of the fine hotels.

On **Lincoln Road** in South Miami Beach is the country's first pedestrian shopping mall, today enjoying a revival as an arts centre. The **Lincoln Road Colony Theater**, the **Miami City Ballet** (where you can watch rehearsals through the shop window) and the **South Florida Art Center** (which houses artists' studios and displays) should not be missed. At the southern tip of Miami Beach is **South Pointe Park** with views across the water to downtown Miami and east out to sea.

### The Islands **

Miami Beach is not just about SoBe, as South Beach is known. Check out **Watson Island**, which was created by dredging in 1931, and pay a visit to the celebrity-studded islands of **Palm**, **Star** and **Hibiscus**, whose residents have included Al Capone (who once lived at 93 Palm Avenue, Palm Island), film stars like Don Johnson at 8 Star Island, and Damon Runyan, whose address was 271 Hibiscus Island. Marvel at the **Morikami Museum** and **Japanese Garden** given to the city in 1961 by Kiyoshi Ichimura, the founder of Ricoh, where focal points are an octagonal pavilion, the Hakkaku-Do, and the eight-ton granite statue of *Hotei*, the smiling god of prosperity. There's also the **Flagler Memorial Monument** and the newly renovated **Bass Museum**

**Above:** *Miami's Art Deco District has become a major tourist attraction.*
**Below:** *Miami Beach teems with visitors throughout the summer.*

**Above:** *An airboat glides through the Everglades.*

**of Art**, which was designed by architect Arata Isozaki and houses a collection of paintings by the Old Masters.

You'll also want to spend time on the beach which stretches 10 miles (16km) down the coast. High-rise hotels line the beaches filled with sun-worshippers. Every available water sport can be tried out before eating or drinking in any of a countless choice of restaurants and bars.

## THE EVERGLADES

Created by the waters of Lake Okeechobee draining slowly towards the sea after the summer rains, the Everglades fill almost all of south Florida between the coasts. With the water usually just a few inches deep and moving imperceptibly through sawgrass plains, the Everglades is aptly described as a 'river of grass'. Studding this low-lying landscape, however, are 'hummocks', tree islands where a slight rise in elevation enables trees to grow and provide a sanctuary for wildlife during the summer floods.

**Everglades National Park** spans 1.4 million acres (566,753ha) but consumes just 20% of the Everglades. Divided into three distinct visitor areas, the park is the best place to explore and comprehend the intricacies of the Everglades, although the area also has several state parks and other visitor-aimed areas, including those offering airboat rides which are popular but regarded as environmentally destructive and not permitted within the national park.

Each section of Everglades National Park can occupy a full-day, although an admission ticket is valid for use at any or all on the same day. The park is open all year but the mosquitoes and storms of summer make winter the prime time to visit. Flamingo is the closest section of the park to Miami, easily accessed off Highway 1. On the approach is the **Ernest Coe Visitor Center**, the largest of several park visitor centres and meriting a call even if you are not visiting this section of the park. From the centre, a 38-mile (98km) road continues into the park with clearly marked stop-points indicating rewarding short walking trails. Several of these pass through small forests of pine or palm, others such as the **Anhinga Trail**, are designed to bring views of wildlife. Another, **Pa-hay-okee Overlook**, reveals a vast expanse of sawgrass dotted by hammocks: the typical Everglades landscape. At the end of the route is dot-on-the-map **Flamingo**, established by hardy settlers in the 1890s. Here there are several short trails and guided walks and canoe trips, as well as the park's only (winter only) hotel. Further west, 35 miles (92km) from Miami off Highway-41, is **Shark Valley** where a two-hour narrated tram tour on a 15-mile (24.14km) loop road provides an excellent introduction to the Everglades, its seasonal cycles and its wildlife. On the route, an observation tower above a pond provides a good vantage point observing turtles, otters, a variety of birdlife and the ubiquitous alligators.

Much closer to Southwest Florida than Miami, **Ten Thousand Islands** is the best section of the park for boat or canoe exploration. Branching off Highway-41 forty miles from Shark Valley, Highway-29 passes first through the white-painted buildings of **Everglades City** before continuing to **Chokoloskee** where the land dissolves into a mangrove-fringed shoreline. From the small docks, boat tours voyage around the innumerable islands that define this section of the park, excellent for viewing birdlife and learning something of pioneer-era life.

The Miccosukee people have lived in the Everglades for many generations. On Highway 41 close to Shark Valley, the **Miccosukee Indian Village** displays handicrafts and cultural artefacts and mounts alligator wrestling shows.

## ALLIGATORS

The largest reptile in North America, the male *Alligator mississippiensis*, can grow up to 16ft (5m). The female is slightly smaller, measuring just under 8ft (2.4m). Alligators are cold-blooded creatures and need to lie in the sun to warm up enough to move. Once mobile they can develop surprising speed. As winter approaches, the rainy season ends and each alligator carves out a 'gator hole'. This hole, filled with underground water, conceals the lurking reptile as it lies in wait for thirsty prey such as deer, raccoons, otters and even birds.

**Below:** *The Everglade swamps are a perfect habitat for alligators.*

## LAUDERDALE ATTRACTIONS

**\* Ah-Tha-Thi-Ki Museum:** explore the cultural heritage of the Seminole Indians in Fort Lauderdale.

**\* Wannado City:** Educational children's theme park where they can try their hand at more than 200 jobs and earn 'Wongas' which they can spend or pay into the bank.

**\*\* Billie Swamp Safari:** interesting swamp buggy rides with Indian guides through the Big Cypress Seminole Indian Reservation.

**\* Butterfly World:** three acres (1.2ha) of tropical garden filled with thousands of colourful butterflies.

**\*\* Flamingo Gardens:** 1½-mile (2.4km) guided tram tour of Florida's wetlands.

**\*\* Sawgrass Recreation Park:** educational glimpse of Indian life, with airboat rides and thrilling alligator shows.

A less traditional venture is the Las Vegas-style Miccosukee hotel and casino (signposted off Highway-41 immediately west of Miami), owned and run by the tribe, which opened in 1999.

## FORT LAUDERDALE

The capital of Broward County was named after Major William Lauderdale who established a fort here in 1838, during the Seminole Indian wars. Until 1911 there were just 175 residents and it was not until the boom years of the 1920s that it became more than a dot on the map.

After 1960 this resort developed a huge following among America's students who headed to the city in their thousands for their traditional spring break. The riotous success of these holidays put off many of the more sedate tourists and eventually the city chiefs forced the students on. Today it is considered one of the top family destinations with its 23 miles (37km) of beach and average year-round temperature of 77°F (25°C).

### Downtown \*\*

One way Fort Lauderdale shed its reputation for student hedonism was by raising its cultural profile and developing the attractive **Riverwalk**, a river-side pathway lined by sculpture and picnic stops that links much of historic Fort Lauderdale with newer attractions such as the **Museum of Discovery and Science** (tel: (954) 467 6637). Here, interactive exhibits are certain to delight children and also educate a few of their parents into the ways of the natural world and beyond: not least with a simulated trip to the moon. Also in Downtown is the 1901 **Stranahan House**, providing revealing insights into the lifestyles of frontier times, and the **Museum of Art**, amongst the diverse stock of which is the US's premier collection works by the influential 1950s European CoBrA movement.

**Below:** *Rollerbladers and joggers enjoy the promenade in Fort Lauderdale.*

From Downtown, the palm-lined **Las Olas Boulevard** runs three miles (4.83km) to the coast lined by some of Fort Lauderdale's most upmarket shops and some of its most expensive homes. The latter occupy the waterside area known as **The Isles**, where the family car typically sits in the driveway while the family yacht is tethered at the rear. From Downtown, shuttle buses run the 12 miles to **Sawgrass Mills**, where more than 350 shops promising goods at less than normal retail prices make this one of the world's largest discount shopping malls.

## The Coast ★★

At its eastern end, Las Olas Boulevard expires directly opposite the Florida beach of a thousand postcards: golden sands fringed by blue ocean waters with palm trees offering vital shade from the sun. This idyllic scene stretches for several miles and accounts for the many small motels lining the side roads and the major hotels grouped at the southern end.

Aside from the glorious beach, coastal Fort Lauderdale also offers the **International Swimming Hall of Fame** (tel: (954) 462 6536), a short walk south of The Strip. This shrine to water sports is packed with medals and trophies of current and former champions, and oddities such as a stock of vintage swimming costumes and photos of a youthful Ronald Reagan during his time as a lifeguard.

Immediately north of the Strip, the **Hugh Taylor Birch State Park** occupies 180 bucolic acres (72.85ha) laced by walking trails beside a pine-fringed lagoon dotted with perfect picnic spots.

> ### WATER TAXIS
>
> One of the easiest ways to get around Fort Lauderdale is by boat, thanks to more than 170 miles (274km) of canals and waterways.
> **Water taxis** have set routes but operate on demand like shared land taxis and can provide a city tour with a difference. Fares start at US$7 per adult for a shuttle fare to US$15 for an all-day pass. For bookings contact: Water taxi, 651 Seabreeze Blvd, tel: (954) 467-6677. Alternatively, you can charter a boat which holds up to 27 passengers (around US$80 for an hour) to take you wherever you want to go.

**Left:** Fort Lauderdale's Swimming Hall of Fame is a monument to sunshine and fine weather.

**Opposite:** *Polo is one of the favourite sports in upmarket Palm Beach.*
**Below:** *Whitehall was railroad magnate Henry Flagler's Palm Beach home.*

More tranquil gardens surround the nearby **Bonnet House**, a plantation-style abode built in the 1920s and open to visitors for worthwhile guided tours: tel: (954) 524 4736.

## PALM BEACH COUNTY

South of Palm Beach lies lovely **Boca Raton** which claims to be one of Florida's most attractive cities with its Spanish Revival style and 5 miles (8km) of glorious oceanfront. **Delray Beach**, a little further on, is worth a visit just for the Japanese Gardens and interesting Morikami Museum of Japanese Culture. The 200-acre (81ha) garden is famed for its bonsai which include the only known collection of Floridian bonsai plants. It also houses a Shinto shrine, a traditional Japanese teahouse and some picnic pavilions, as well as a recently added audiovisual exhibit about Japanese culture.

### Palm Beach ★★★

**Palm Beach** itself was created as an exclusive resort for the rich and famous and, more than a hundred years on, has retained its distinguished air. Less than 70 miles (112km) north of Miami, it is light years away in style and atmosphere. City centre bustle is replaced by elegant calm. Like so much of southern Florida, Palm Beach owes its success to railroad king **Henry Flagler**, since it was the first town that he developed on the east coast of Florida. He was helped by architect **Addison Mizner**, who had been commissioned by some of America's wealthiest – the Vanderbilts, the Whitneys and the Wanamakers – after an enormously successful debut with the Everglades Club on Worth Avenue. **Whitehall**, Henry Flagler's magnificent and imposing home, still stands on Coconut Row in Palm Beach and is now open as a museum filled with many original furnishings and even a private railway car. Other attractions also include an

impressive art collection, complete with a masterful Gainsborough, as well as a 1200-pipe organ and unusual architecture – the dining room ceiling is a stunning combination of gilded wood carving and papier-mâché. Tel: (561) 655-2833. After visiting the home of the man who made the dream come true, take a trip down exclusive **Worth Avenue** and watch as millions of dollars exchange hands for top fashion, jewellery and toys.

This is the town to catch up on your polo. There are three grounds for you to choose from and some games are free to watch. Alternatively, head out to play on one of the county's 145 golf courses or indulge in a game of croquet – Palm Beach is home to the National Croquet Center.

Palm Beach County offers about 47 miles (75km) of beach with great water sports facilities. Five species of turtle along with thousands of coral reef fish occur along this shoreline – and, because this is Palm Beach, a 1967 Rolls Royce Silver Shadow, purposely sunken to provide an 'upmarket' dive site.

## West Palm Beach ★

Across the water from Palm Beach is the largest city in the county, West Palm Beach, home to the **Kravis Cultural Center** as well as the **Dreher Park Zoo** and the **Norton Gallery of Art** and **Norton Sculpture Gardens** – which are probably visited more for their botanical appeal (indigenous plants, including 300 species of palms, attract prolific birdlife).

The **South Florida Science Museum** features hands-on exhibits for all ages, an aquarium and planetarium shows. It also houses southern Florida's most powerful telescope, with night-sky viewing on Fridays if the weather permits.

Opened in 2002, **Cityplace** (www.cityplace.com) is a great place to shop, eat and drink and there is always plenty of evening entertainment too.

### POLO

Polo matches are held in West Palm Beach. Celebrities and the wealthy frequently attend to watch a *chukka* (7½ minutes of continuous play) and sip champagne.
If you want to watch try:
**Gulf Stream Polo Club**, tel: (561) 965-2057.
No admission fee for Friday and Sunday games, December–April.
**Royal Palm Polo**, tel: (561) 994-1876.
Games played on Sundays, June–October, January–April.
**Palm Beach Polo and Country Club**, tel: (561) 793-1440. Host of the World Cup (April). Prince Charles used to play here.

The **Lion Country Safari** west of town is a 500-acre (202ha) complex where lions, giraffes, elephants, antelope and zebras roam free. Ensure that you arrive early in order to beat the crowds.

Just down the road from the Lion Country Safari is the **Arthur R Marshall Loxahatchee National Wildlife Reserve**, which forms part of the northern Everglades. This untouched wilderness area is perfect for walking or canoeing and provides an opportunity for visitors to discover the original Florida.

**Above:** *Classic cars and baseball memorabilia fill the Elliott Museum.*
**Opposite:** *The inland parks offer a wealth of canoeing opportunities.*

## MARTIN COUNTY

Travelling north from Palm Beach the slick tourist resorts dwindle into a wilderness of river swamps, mangrove forests and offshore islands. Towns are replaced by wildlife refuges and conservation areas lining Florida's largest inland waterway, Lake Okeechobee.

**Stuart**, the major town in Martin County, was founded in the 1880s and is a mecca for fresh- and saltwater anglers. Sights in the town include the **Elliott Museum** built by inventor Harmon Parker Elliott. Inside, a baseball hall of fame contains memorabilia of Babe Ruth and Ty Cobb, though the museum's real attraction is its treasure trove of gizmos. Elliott and his father Sterling claimed more than 200 patents, and early examples of their wizardry are on display, including an early version of an answering machine. It also houses a substantial collection of bicycles, motorcycles and cars – there's even a 1922 Rolls Royce Pall Mall Phantom. Open 13:00–16:00 daily.

**Gilbert's Bar House of Refuge**, named after the offshore reef that caused many shipwrecks in earlier centuries, was once a haven for shipwrecked sailors. It now houses mementos of early seafaring days.

---

### LAKE OKEECHOBEE

Lake Okeechobee, on the western fringes of Palm Beach County, covers 448,000 acres (181,303ha). It is the fourth-largest natural lake in the United States yet is rarely more than 16ft (5m) deep. Although the lake is a mecca for fishermen, facilities for other activities are limited. **Pahokee** and **Belle Glade** have marinas and boat ramps. The lake traditionally drains into the Everglades, providing nutrient-rich waters for the swamps. Drainage for agricultural purposes has led to fierce clashes between farmers and environmentalists. Farmers need the water for their lands, while environmentalists maintain that the swamps should be left undisturbed.

## Outdoors **

Almost opposite the Elliott Museum is the 40-acre (16ha) **Coastal Science Center** operated by the Florida Oceanographic Society, with interesting displays on coastal ecology as well as several nature trails.

Massive **Jonathan Dickinson State Park** covers 11,300 acres (4573ha). Visitors can roam paths leading through scrub, flatwoods, mangroves and river swamps or take a tour down Florida's only designated wild river, the Loxahatchee. Guides can be booked through the **Trapper Nelson Interpretive Site**, named after a man who lived in these wilds for almost 40 years. You can also book canoe trips, horse-riding trails and overnight cabins. For general park information tel: (561) 546-2771.

At nearby Hobe Sound, the **St Lucie Inlet State Preserve** is accessible only by private boat. A 1094yd (1000m) boardwalk takes visitors through mangrove forests out to miles of sandy beach. Each summer the area becomes home to nesting loggerhead, green and leatherback turtles, as well as a screeching profusion of seabirds. The offshore reefs are popular with snorkellers and scuba divers for their colourful corals, myriad tropical fish and, occasionally, a glimpse of a turtle.

### St Lucie County

North of Stuart lies the old town of **Fort Pierce**, where you'll find the **St Lucie County Historical Museum**. It contains many early 20th-century military artefacts as well as a Spanish treasure room. But the real purpose of a visit is the **Fort Pierce Inlet State Recreation Area**. A sandy ocean floor and good Atlantic waves make this a choice surfing spot, while the windswept dunes and coastal hummocks provide interesting nature trails.

---

**FINDERS KEEPERS**

Some 1800 ships are believed to have sunk along Florida's **Treasure Coast** during the 16th and 17th centuries. Laden **Spanish galleons** on their way from the New World back to Europe were prime targets for the British fleet and pirates alike. Vessels also fell prey to sudden, severe storms and treacherous reefs. The most famous recovery of gold and jewels occurred in 1985, when **Mel Fisher** recovered US$100 million of booty from the *Atocha* and *La Margarita*. Experts estimate that there is another US$250 million worth of sunken treasure to salvage.

# The Southeast at a Glance

## BEST TIMES TO VISIT

With temperatures rarely dropping below 60°F (16°C), southeast Florida is popular both summer and winter. In the hotter but less busy **summer** months, **tropical thunderstorms** herald the arrival of dense swarms of mosquitoes. Southern Florida lies in the **hurricane belt** and is most likely to be hit during **September/October**.

## GETTING THERE

**Miami International Airport**, tel: (305) 876-7077, 6 miles (10km) from the downtown area, is the major gateway to the region with hundreds of flights arriving daily from Europe, the United States, the Caribbean and South America.

Free **shuttle buses** run between the airport and hotels in the area.

There are also **Metrobus** and **Greyhound** services from the airport.

Most **car rental** firms are represented at the airport. **Fort Lauderdale–Hollywood International Airport**, tel: (954) 359-6111, and **Palm Beach International Airport**, tel: (561) 471-7400, both offer good domestic connections.

Again, hotels offer shuttle services and there are plenty of taxis.

**Gray Line**, tel: (305) 561-8886, operates shared-ride and private car service.

## GETTING AROUND

Driving south down Florida's **Turnpike** is the best route by car. **Greyhound** has bus services into southern Florida, and **Amtrak** offers trains direct from New York as part of a national network.

**Cruise ships** berth in Miami, Fort Lauderdale and Palm Beach.

**Car hire** can be very good value in Florida and is often a cheaper alternative to relying on taxis if you are planning more than the odd day out. The **Metromover** in Miami provides good downtown transport while **Metrobuses** operate across the greater Miami area, backed by **Metrorail** operations.

Fort Lauderdale's land-based transport system is supported by an extensive network of **water taxis**.

**Cabs** (taxis) are easy to flag down and usually congregate around hotels.

## WHERE TO STAY

### Miami/Miami Beach
*LUXURY*

**Mandarin Oriental Miami**, 601 Brickell Key DR, tel: (305) 373-0141, web: www. mandarinoriental.com/miami/ Top-class hotel from this international five-star brand.

**The Biltmore Hotel**, 1200 Anastasia Avenue, Coral Gables, tel: (305) 445-8066, fax: 913-3159, or website: www.biltmorehotel.com A luxurious top-class hotel.

*MID-RANGE*

**Miami International Airport Hotel**, PO Box 997510, Airport Terminal Concourse E Miami, Florida 33299-7510, tel: (305) 871-4100, fax: 871-0800, web: www.miahotel. com Inside the airport terminal, perfect for over-nighting before early flights.

**Indian Creek Hotel**, 2727 Indian Creek Dr, Miami Beach, toll-free: (800) 491 2772, fax: (305) 531-5651, web: www.indiancreekhotel. com Comfortable 1930s hotel.

*BUDGET*

**Miami Beach Resort & Spa**, 4833 Collins Ave, Miami Beach, FL33140, tel: (305) 532-3600, fax: (305) 534-7409. In the heart of the Art Deco District.

### Fort Lauderdale
*LUXURY*

**Radisson Bahia Mar Beach Resort**, 801 Seabreeze Blvd, tel: (954) 764-2233, fax: 524-6912. Across the road from the ocean.

*MID-RANGE*

**Best Western Oceanside Inn**, 1180 Seabreeze Blvd, tel: (954) 525-8115, fax: 527-0957, web: www.book bestwestern.com A stone's throw from the ocean; breakfast is included.

*BUDGET*

**Travelodge**, 4011 N Ocean Blvd, tel: (954) 763-6601,

web: www.travelodge.com
Local branch of nationwide low-priced hotels well-placed for beachside Fort Lauderdale. The rate includes free morning coffee, a free newspaper and free Cable TV service.

### Palm Beach

#### LUXURY
**The Breakers**, One South Country Road, Palm Beach, tel: (561) 655-6611, fax: (561) 659-8403, web: www.the breakers.com The ultimate in glitz and glamour.

#### MID-RANGE
**Heart of Palm**, 160 Royal Palm Way, tel: (407) 655-5600. Walking distance to ocean. Value for money in an otherwise expensive town.

#### BUDGET
**Days Inn**, 2300 45th Street, West Palm Beach, tel: (800) 352-6786, web: www.days inn.com Hotel chain offering basic facilities at low cost.

### WHERE TO EAT

### Miami
**Blue Door at Delano**, 1685 Collins Ave, Miami Beach, tel: (305) 674-6400. French-Brazilian cuisine.
**Smith & Wollensky**, 1 Washington Ave, Miami Beach, tel: (305) 673-2800, American dining; reservations recommended.
**La Carreta**, 3632 SW Eighth Street, tel: (305) 444-7501.

Cheap Cuban restaurant in the heart of Little Havana.
**P. F. Chang's China Bistro**, 901 S Miami Ave, Miami, tel: (305) 358-0731. One of 130 in the chain nationwide with good reviews.

### Fort Lauderdale
**Mai-Kai**, 3599 N Federal Highway, tel: (954) 583-3272, web: www. maikai.com Specializes in Polynesian food.
**15th Street Fisheries**, 1900 SE 15th St, tel: (954) 763-2777. Old Florida style seafood restaurant with a $9 lunch, and pricier dinner with everything from shrimp to kangaroo and alligator.

### Palm Beach
**The Breakers**, 1 S County Road, tel: (561) 655-6611. Reservations required; dress smartly for this famous hotel.

### TOURS AND EXCURSIONS
**Everglades Safari Park**, 26700 Tamiami Trl, Miami, tel: (305) 226-6923, web: www.evsafaripark.com Guided airboat tours through the glades.

**Sea Experience**, 801 Seabreeze Blvd, Fort Lauderdale, tel (954) 467-6000, web: www.seaxp.com Snorkel or ride in a glass-bottom boat above coral reefs.
**Island Queen Sightseeing Tours**, 401 Biscayne Rd, Miami, tel: 0800-910-5119, web: www.islandqueen cruises.com Take a ride along Miami's coastline

### USEFUL CONTACTS
**Greater Miami Convention & Visitors Bureau**, 701 Brickell Ave, tel: (305) 539-3000, web: www.miamiand beaches.com
**Greater Fort Lauderdale Convention & Visitors Bureau**, 1850 Eller Dr, tel: (954) 765-4466, web: www.sunny.org
**Palm Beach County Convention & Visitors Bureau**, 1555 Palm Beach Lakes Blvd, tel: (561) 233-3000, web: www.palm beachfl.com
**Tropical Everglades Visitor Association**, 160 US Hway 1, Homestead, tel: 0800-388-9669, web: www.tropical everglades.com

| MIAMI | J | F | M | A | M | J | J | A | S | O | N | D |
|---|---|---|---|---|---|---|---|---|---|---|---|---|
| AVERAGE TEMP. °F | 67 | 68 | 72 | 75 | 78 | 81 | 82 | 83 | 82 | 79 | 73 | 68 |
| AVERAGE TEMP. °C | 15 | 16 | 18 | 20 | 22 | 24 | 24 | 25 | 24 | 22 | 19 | 16 |
| HOURS OF SUN DAILY | 12 | 12 | 12 | 13 | 13 | 14 | 14 | 14 | 13 | 12 | 12 | 12 |
| RAINFALL in | 2 | 2 | 2 | 3 | 6.5 | 9 | 6 | 7 | 8 | 7 | 2.5 | 2 |
| RAINFALL mm | 51 | 51 | 51 | 76 | 165 | 229 | 152 | 179 | 203 | 179 | 63 | 51 |
| DAYS OF RAINFALL | 7 | 7 | 7 | 8 | 12 | 15 | 12 | 13 | 14 | 13 | 8 | 7 |

# 3
# Orlando and
# Central Florida

A dream come true for young and old alike, a dazzling fantasy land where everything is fun, where happy children play and carefree adults laugh – this is the home of **Mickey Mouse**, probably the most concentrated theme park area in the world. Whether you want to watch an alligator wrestling match, hug Minnie Mouse, eat out in the Wild West, or get your adrenaline pumping on daring rides, it is all possible here.

Take your pick from the delightful splendours of the **Magic Kingdom**® and educational **Epcot**®, the thrills of **Universal Studios**® or **Wet 'n Wild**® and **SeaWorld**® **Orlando**. In an area where development really started only 100 years ago, the fun doesn't stop when the sun sets. Most theme parks are located in **Orlando** and on the road south towards **Kissimmee**. Many visitors fly straight to Orlando and then cherry-pick other attractions.

There are some choice **hotels** inside the Walt Disney World® complex, where you can share your cornflakes with Mickey Mouse; or look for movie star magic at the Universal Studios® properties. Alternatively you may prefer the cheaper option and stay slightly further away.

If you need to dilute the intensity of the parks, there are several tempting options. Why not explore the elegant shops of Orlando's **Winter Park**, or nearby Kissimmee which retains its cowboy style of old and hosts the **Silver Spurs Rodeo** in February and October each year. Admire the thoroughbred racehorses of **Ocala** or frolic in the shimmering lakes of **Lake County**. And to the south lies scenic **Polk County**, fragrant heart of the citrus belt.

## DON'T MISS

★★★ **Magic Kingdom**®: the reason most people visit Florida – the home of Mickey Mouse.
★★★ **Universal Studios**®: classic films come to life with special effect rides.
★★★ **CityWalk**: the place to find restaurants, bars and evening entertainment
★★ **SeaWorld**®: with white knuckle rides and close encounters with creatures of the deep.
★★ **Wet 'n Wild**®: the very best way to cool off from the Florida heat.

**Opposite:** *Lazy River, Wet 'n Wild*®, *is one of Orlando's less hair-raising attractions.*

Central Florida

## ORLANDO

The city of Orlando, now some 120 years old, was little more than a military outpost until 1875.

It is believed to have been named after **Orlando Reeves**, a soldier who was killed by an Indian arrow while on duty back in 1835. Agriculture dominated the early development, due to a year-round sunny, warm climate and the area's central position in the state. Almost 50 years ago, corporations began to arrive and the city started to blossom into the thriving metropolis it is today.

The reason that brings most people to this area is the winning combination of Mickey Mouse and Universal Studios® in an area liberally dotted with theme parks and attractions. **Orlando International Airport** receives numerous direct scheduled flights from Europe, while Orlando Sanford Airport receives the international charter traffic.

It comes almost as a shock to find that Disney does not own the entire territory, so formidable has the image of the little mouse become, but theme parks aside, the downtown area offers an abundance of other interesting diversions. Sports fans, too, are well catered for. **Golfers** will be delighted to find 135 golf courses (at the last count) within 45 minutes of the city (more than 100 courses within the Greater Orlando area). Course designers include Joe Lee, Tom Fazio, Robert Trent Jones, Greg Norman, Tom Watson and Jack Nicklaus. Others like Nick Price, Gary Player and Arnold Palmer all have homes in the city,

## CLIMATE

The **hottest** months are from **July** to **September** when the average highs reach 91°F (33°C), but temperatures can reach 80°F (27°C) between April and June. **Winters** are **milder** with temperatures a pleasant average of 74°F (23°C) and above.

which hosts at least four major tournaments a year. More than 800 **tennis courts** are available and spectators can choose between basketball's Orlando Magic and American football's Orlando Predators.

**Charles Hosmer Morse Museum of American Art** ★
This museum in Winter Park is home to the world's most comprehensive collection of works by Louis Comfort Tiffany, including many of his most recognised windows, lamps and vases as well as jewellery, paintings and furniture.

**Above:** *Park Avenue in Winter Park is lined with glitzy boutiques and chic pavement cafés.*

**Mennello Museum of American Folk Art** ★
Florida's only museum dedicated to exhibiting the works of self-taught artists, including renowned folk artist Earl Cunningham.

**Albin Polasek Museum & Sculpture Gardens** ★
Listed on the National Register of Historic Places, this museum showcases nearly 200 of Czech-American sculptor Albin Polasek's sculptures and paintings.

**Zora Neale Hurston National Museum of Fine Arts** ★
Named for the renowned African-American writer, folklorist and anthropologist, this museum celebrates works by African artists. Hurston is also commemorated through an annual arts and humanities festival held in her hometown of Eatonville, just north of downtown Orlando.

**Orlando Museum of Art** ★★
This museum at 2416 North Mills Avenue, Loch Haven Park, has a permanent collection of 19th- and 20th-century works, Mayan artefacts and a delightful 'Art Encounter', aimed at children. Its permanent *Art of the Ancient Americas Collection* includes more than 750 pieces of

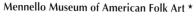

## WINDING DOWN

After a few hard days in the parks, Orlando has a variety of spa resorts for the ultimate pampering. **Wyndham Palace Resort & Spa** and **The Greenhouse Spa** at the Portofino Bay Hotel are inside the Disney and Universal parks respectively while the newest and largest is the **Ritz-Carlton Spa**, Grand Lakes Orlando. Two more are due to open in autumn 2004, the **Regent Winter Park** and the **Omni Orlando Resort** at ChampionsGate.

## THEME PARK TIPS

There is so much to do in Orlando that it is well worth your while planning ahead. Here are a few key pointers:

• Don't cram too much activity into one day.

• If you stay inside the park, you can start on the rides one hour ahead of the crowds.

• Use Fasttrack passes at Disney and Express passes at Universal (shorter queing time).

• If you have young children, hire a pushchair or quit early.

• Be prepared to queue, particularly in peak summer.

• Wear hats to minimize a risk of sunburn or heatstroke.

• Save time by choosing your priority rides and planning a sensible route between them.

• Don't spend days in a row in the parks; take breaks.

• Be warned – every park is a kid's heaven of sweet and gift shops. Don't expect to leave empty-handed.

ancient art from 30 different cultural groups in North, Central and South America. It is considered to be the broadest and most representative collection in the Southeast United States.

## THEME PARKS

Theme parks abound in and around Orlando. Here we give you a snapshot of some of the best.

## WALT DISNEY WORLD® RESORT

Walt Disney World® Resort is a massive complex of theme parks and housing four theme parks, two water parks, resort hotels, 99 holes of golf on six courses, two full-service spas, Disney's wedding pavilion, Disney's Wide World of Sports® complex and Downtown Disney®, an entertainment, shopping and dining complex (www.disneyworld.co.uk).

### The Magic Kingdom® ★★★

For many people this park epitomizes Walt Disney World® and, with more than 40 major rides and shows spread across a 107-acre site, is the first stop on any visit. Call tel: (407) 824-4321 for opening times. Enchanting **Cinderella Castle** lies at the heart of the Magic Kingdom®, its seven themed lands radiating outward like the spokes of a wheel. **Main Street USA**, lined with old-time shops and restaurants, leads you from the main entrance to the castle and is the site of the daily **Parade** at 15:00.

    **Adventureland** is home to the quaint **Swiss Family Treehouse**, the sweet tunes of the **Enchanted Tiki Birds**, a steamy **Jungle Cruise** and the **Extraterrorestial Alien Encounter**. The pace picks up a bit in **Frontierland®** where you will encounter the first white-knuckle ride – the world's longest flume drop from **Splash Mountain®** – as well as the slightly tamer **Big Thunder Mountain Railroad** and **Tom Sawyer Island**. **Liberty Square** takes a look back at America's history. Take a steamboat ride and visit the interesting

Hall of Presidents and the spooky **Haunted Mansion** filled with cobwebs, apparitions and creepy sounds.

This is also home to the last attraction which was personally overseen by Walt Disney himself but which has come to worldwide fame in the past few years thanks to Johnny Depp and his alter ego Captain Jack Sparrow. The ride **Pirates of the Caribbean** has now spawned two films with a third on its way and is high on the list of the 'must do' rides.

**Fantasyland** is perfect for little visitors, offering Peter Pan, Dumbo, Mad Hatter's Tea Party and Snow White rides and carousels, and the singing dolls of **It's a Small World**. Among the new highlights is **Mickey's PhilharMagic** where guests can be dazzled by Mickey Mouse, Donald Duck and the other Disney favourites in a hilarious adventure through movies, music and mayhem.

**Mickey's Toontown Fair** is where you'll find Mickey and his friends in a cartoon world brought to life. Stroll along the **Walk of Fame**, where characters' voices are activated by stepping on the stars.

Older visitors will not want to skip **Tomorrowland**® and its highlight ride, **Space Mountain**®, an unnerving roller coaster in the dark. Nervous visitors may prefer the calmer **Grand Prix Raceway**, which is really aimed at children. 2007 also saw the opening of the new **Monster Inc Comedy Club** where children can help Mike Wazowski, your 'Monster of Ceremonies', and his wild and crazy pals

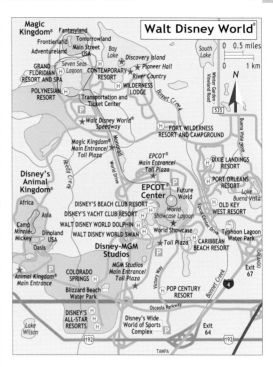

**Opposite:** *Fireworks light up the night sky at Disney's Magic Kingdom®.*

---

**TOP DISNEY RIDES**

Classic Disney rides include:
• Pirates of the Caribbean, Magic Kingdom®
• Splash Mountain®, Magic Kingdom®
• The Haunted Mansion, Magic Kingdom®
• Kilimanjaro Safaris®, Disney's Animal Kingdom®
• Honey, I shrunk the Audience, Epcot® Center

**Right:** *The high-tech wizardry at Epcot® impresses young and old alike.*

power the city of Monstropolis – with laughter! And another new attraction in Tomorrowland® is **Stitch's Great Escape**™ where guests report for duty as a new security recruit in the Galactic Federation Prisoner Teleport Center to guard Experiment 626, the six-limbed alien known as 'Stitch' with an appetite for chaos and the uncanny ability to wreak havoc wherever he goes.

### Disney's Animal Kingdom® ★★★

A mix of safari and theme park, this attraction first opened its doors in 1998 and has been growing ever since.

At the heart of the park lies the 50-foot wide Tree of Life® with its 325 animal carvings. Disney has devised a series of animal encounter adventures including the **Affection Section**, where children can get close to a selection of furry creatures from bunnies and sheep to llamas, and the more exotic **Maharajah Jungle Trek**® where you can watch tigers and tapirs, or the **Pangani Forest Exploration Trail**® which promises a nature walk through an African valley filled with Nile hippos, birds and fish. Watch the hippos from an underwater viewing area and have a close-up encounter with a troop of gorillas.

By contrast, the other areas are much more like a traditional theme park with big thrills including the **Dinosaur ride** back through time to rescue a stray dinoasaur, or the new Expedition Everest™ – **Legend of the Forbidden Mountain™**. There is plenty of fun for the little ones, including the new **TriceraTop Spin**, the **Wildlife Express Train** and **The Boneyard®**.

For the slightly more adventurous there are the **Kali River Rapids®** and the new **Primeval Whirl®** – a spinning roller coaster.

### Epcot® ★★★

Covering 260 acres and split into two areas, Epcot® is divided between **Future World** focusing on discovery and scientific achievements and **World Showcase** reflecting the cultures of the world. Mission Space and Test Track are among the top attractions, along with The Twilight Zone Tower of Terror™, while more recent additions include **The Seas with Nemo and Friends** and the big thrills of **Mission: Space and Soarin'**.

### Disney-MGM Studios ★★

A working film, TV, radio and animation studio that was home to the making of *Lilo and Stitch* as well as a theme park featuring more than 20 rides, attractions and shows. New attractions include a walk through the wardrobe into Narnia, as well as two new shows, **Playhouse Disney™** and **Lights, Motors, Action!™ – Extreme Stunt Show**.

### Disney Water Parks ★★

Disney has two water parks – **Blizzard Beach** and **Typhoon Lagoon**. Escape to the watery wonderland at Blizzard Beach where the big thrills include a Slush Gusher and Summit Plummet and the milder rides include Runoff Rapids and Snow Stormers. Or travel to Typhoon Lagoon where you can choose between the thrill of Shark Reef and Mayda Falls or travel gently down an amazing 610m (2000ft) river ride. The latest attraction is the **Crush 'n Gusher**, with jets of water rushing your raft through down the roller coaster.

---

### SHOPPING

Shopaholics beware – retail space abounds in Orlando:
• Altamonte Mall, Osceola Square, Orlando Fashion Square, Seminole Town Center.
• Belz Factory Outlet World: more than 160 discount stores.
• Orlando's Antique Row.
• Mall at Millenia, Orlando: for high end shopping.
• Downtown Kissimmee and St Cloud: antique shopping galore.
• Park Avenue: upmarket boutiques in Winter Park.
• Theme parks: wide variety of merchandise for sale.
• Downtown Disney® and CityWalk.
• Airport: last-minute souvenirs.

**Right:** *Universal Studios® offers rides, stunt shows and movie memorabilia.* **Opposite:** *Killer whales perform daily at SeaWorld® Orlando.*

### OUTSIDE DISNEY

### Universal Studios® ★★★

A worthy rival for the Disney empire, no visit to Orlando would be complete without experiencing the fabulous shows, rides and thrills of Universal Studios®. The Studios, located at 1000 Universal Studios Plaza, are open from 09:00 daily.

**Terminator 2: Battle Across Time** is billed as the world's first 4D, interactive attraction. Also do not miss **Earthquake**, **Jaws**, **Back to the Future**, **Twister**, **Shrek 4D**, or **The Revenge of the Mummy**, all of which are guaranteed to cause sweaty palms, shrieks and palpitations.

Adjacent to Universal Studios® is Universal's second park, **Islands Of Adventure**. This excellent park features two of the world's best roller-coaster rides, **Duelling Dragons** and the **Incredible Hulk Coaster**, as well as the 3D ride – **Amazing Adventure of Spiderman**. Try out **The Flying Unicorn** and **Storm Force** on Marvel Super Hero Island or discover the delights of Dr Seuss and his amazing characters. Adjacent to the park is **CityWalk**, with themed restaurants and nightlife venues.

### Wet 'n Wild® Orlando ★★

This theme park at 6200 International Drive has white knuckle rides to challenge even the most hardy of thrill seekers while the whole park has water slides, flumes, lazy rivers and pools to keep water babies of all ages happy for

**OUT IN THE WILDS**

Even the most ardent theme park fan will soon become aware that beyond the domain of Mickey Mouse Florida has many expanses of undeveloped and often untamed land. Be it swamp, forest or prairie, sizeable chunks of the state are variously protected as federally-run national parks, such as Everglades and Biscayne, or Florida-run state parks. Many lesser known areas also enjoy various levels of protection, such as the Lower Suwannee National Wildlife Refuge near Cedar Key and the Timucuan Ecological and Historical Reserve near Jacksonville.

hours. Open year round, though times vary according to season.

### Ripley's Believe It or Not!® Museum ★

A peculiar attraction not to be missed, this rather bizarre museum, also on International Drive, is housed in a strange building made to look as though it is about to sink into a Florida sinkhole and provides odd entertainment for relatively low cost. Open 09:00–01:00 daily.

### SeaWorld® Orlando ★★

Established in 1973, SeaWorld® Orlando, on 7007 SeaWorld Drive, offers the stunning **Wild Arctic**, which combines a flight over the frozen North and close-up encounters with wildlife including polar bears. State-of-the-art rides such as Kraken and Journey to Atlantis vie for your attention with Believe which showcases killer whales performing awe-inspiring choreography all set to stirring music. Open 09:00–19:00 in winter, 09:00–20:00 in spring and autumn, 09:00–23:00 in summer.

### Discovery Cove ★★★

Adjacent to SeaWorld® Orlando is Discovery Cove, where visitors can snorkel through coral reefs with marine animals and swim among dolphins. Reservations are required, tel: 877 4DISCOVERY. Or visit the website: www.discoverycove.com

### Nightlife Attractions ★

Evening entertainment is as varied as the theme parks. Venues are highly competitive and forever trying to outdo one another. They also extend the fantasy flavour of Orlando, from **Makahiki Luau** at SeaWorld® Orlando, where guests are whisked off to Hawaii, to the **Improv Comedy Club and Restaurant** in West Church Street in downtown Orlando with the best stand-up comedians around.

---

#### FISHING

Lake County is named after its 1440 lakes. Many people visit the area in search of peace and quiet after the frenzy of Orlando. Fishing is a popular pastime here, the waters containing some 115 species. The largemouth bass is Florida's official freshwater fish. If you are over 16 years of age you may need a fishing or hunting licence n some parts of the state. For details of local regulations contact the **Florida Game and Fresh Water Fish Commission**, tel: (904) 488-1960 or 488-2975. Kissimee in Osceola County offers some of the best fishing lakes in the United States. The area's Lake Tohopekaliga, or Toho for short, and the Kissimmee Chain of Lakes have produced record breaking fish and annually host several competitions.

**Right:** *Glass-bottom boats travel across Silver Springs in search of alligators, fish and turtles.*

### AROUND ORLANDO

Leaving the glittering illusions of Orlando behind, you discover that central Florida has some unspoilt areas that look much the same now as they must have when discovered by the Europeans a few hundred years ago.

To the east, near the town of Christmas, lies the **Tosohatchee State Reserve**, said to be one of the most pristine sites in the region. Visitors are free to roam through the park, along 40 miles (65km) of the **Florida Trail**. During hunting season you are obliged to wear bright orange warning vests, and it's best to call ahead to warn the park rangers of your arrival. Also to the east of Orlando is an artificial wetland area – the **Orlando Wilderness Park**. This is an excellent place for bird spotting, but is closed during the hunting season, which lasts from 1 October to 20 January.

Heading north from Orlando, you pass through **Maitland**. Visit the popular **Art Center**, which promotes American art and artists in an attractive rural setting. Victoriana rules supreme at the **Historic Waterhouse Residence and Carpentry Shop Museums**, which were built in 1884 and maintain their stately Victorian air to this day. Equally interesting are the **Maitland Historical Museum** and the **Telephone Museum**.

Nostalgia is the key note at **Sanford** where the steamboat, *Grand Romance*, puffs along the St Johns River with up to 350 dinner guests on board.

---

**ANNUAL EVENTS AROUND ORLANDO**

**January** • Florida Citrus Festival and Polk County Fair.
**February** • Silver Spurs Rodeo, held in Kissimmee since 1944.
**March** • Four-day Kissimmee Bluegrass Music Festival.
**April** • Polk City week of aviation events.
**May** • Annual outdoor Art Festival at Lakeland.
**June** • Bi-annual International Orchid Fair, last held 1996.
**October** • Florida Horse and Agricultural Festival, Ocala.
**November** • Chrysanthemum Festival, Cypress Gardens.
**December** • Florida Citrus Sailfest at Lake Monroe.
**Mid-December** • Very Merry Christmas Parade, the Magic Kingdom®, Walt Disney World®.

## Lake County ★

Further to the northwest of Orlando, the St Johns River is joined by the Wekiwa River at Apopka, which is the home of the **Wekiwa Springs State Park**. The numerous tributaries feeding into the river form perfect canoeing trails, while energetic hikers can choose from several splendid, well-mapped paths.

Beyond, and pretty as a postcard, the tiny village of **Mount Dora** perches on top of a bluff overlooking Lake Dora. Many of the quaint cottages decorated with flower-filled window boxes are now art galleries and tempting antique shops, reminiscent of New England rather than Florida. **Renninger's Twin Markets**, held here each week-end, attract up to 500 antique dealers.

**Lake Dora** lies in the heart of Lake County, which was named for its abundance of water. A canal, said to be one of the most beautiful in the world, connects lakes Dora and Eustis and is perfect for relaxing cruises.

Further north, in Marion County, the landscape changes from the typical Florida flatlands to rolling green hills. This lush farmland is filled with cattle and thoroughbred race horses. Some of the 400 horse farms have open days, when visitors can visit the facilities and watch training sessions.

## Ocala ★★

Near Ocala be sure to visit the **Ocala National Forest** with its sand pine trees and **Silver Springs**, one of the state's oldest attractions and the world's largest natural spring. The Springs contain alligators, turtles and largemouth bass. Travel on a glass-bottom boat – the water is so clear here that one can see to a depth of 80ft (24m). Or take an exciting jeep safari or jungle cruise. Children will enjoy the **Wild Waters** next to the park, with its giant wave pool, slides and water cannons. For opening times call tel: (904) 236-2121 or 800 274-7458.

The 350-acre (142ha) **Ocala National Forest** incorporates more than 100 miles (160km) of horse trails and 65 miles (105km) of the Florida National Scenic Trail. One of the most enjoyable ways to experience the park is by

### LAKE TOHOPEKALIGA

Seminole Indians once lived on the shores of this lake which today separates St Cloud and Kissimmee. The lake is also the setting for special events like the annual Kissimmee Bluegrass Music Festival, and the autumn Viva Osceola Latin Music Festival.

leisurely canoe or on horseback. There are also dive and snorkel sites.

Among Ocala's attractions is **The Appleton Museum of Art** with its regularly changing exhibitions of antiquities dating back 5000 years. Here you can marvel at early Rembrandt etchings, a 'Thinker' by Rodin (cast from the *original* mould), Turkish prayer rugs, a wooden Tibetan saddle and Japanese figurines. Open 10:00–16:30 Tuesday–Saturday, 13:00–17:00 Sunday.

The distinctly 20th-century **Don Garlits Museum of Drag Racing** houses a collection of antique cars, as well as the famous 'swamp rats' (specialized drag racing vehicles). Open 09:00–17:30 daily, except Christmas Day.

**Above:** *Kissimmee is cowboy country, and rodeos are held regularly.*

## Clermont ★

Clermont, to the west of Orlando, is home to the fascinating **House of Presidents Wax Museum**. Figures range from George Washington to Bill Clinton. It is also at the centre of Florida's wine production, and vineyards carpet the landscape. With the help and advice of the nearby University of Florida, the region now produces very palatable wines. **Lakeridge Winery and Vineyards** is open to the public for wine-tasting and tours. The other main crop around Clermont is citrus fruit and from the **Florida Citrus Tower** on Highway 27 you can enjoy a stunning panoramic view across the region.

## Kissimmee ★★

Within easy driving of Orlando, the Kissimmee area offers plenty of themed entertainment, while managing to retain old-world charm. The emphasis here is on cowboys, rodeos and the outdoors rather than Mickey Mouse, but the hotels are happy to sell themselves as the perfect spot from which to explore Walt Disney World®, just a few miles north.

**Left:** *The safest way to see alligators is at Gatorland south of Orlando.*

Kissimmee is slightly closer to Walt Disney World®, lying on the northwestern tip of **Lake Tohopekaliga**, while St Cloud lies just a few kilometres to the east on the southern shores of **East Lake Tohopekaliga**.

As you head south from Orlando along S Orange Blossom Trail, **Gatorland** is worth a stop to shiver at the sight of more than 5000 prehistoric-looking alligators. The park has thrilling daily shows such as Gator Jumparoo, Gator Wrestling and Snakes Alive, and a restaurant where gator ribs are on the menu. Open 09:00–17:00. Friendlier animals are found at the **Green Meadows Petting Farm**, which provides a two-hour tour of 300 farm animals, with younger visitors being encouraged to touch. Open 09:30–17:30 daily.

Along Highway 192, Kissimmee's main thoroughfare, you will find the charming town of **Celebration**. This much publicised Disney-planned residential community is intended to recapture the spirit of small-town America.

**Warbird Adventures** at 233 Hoagland Boulevard offers wannabe fighter pilots an opportunity to fly vintage World War II aircraft.

The **World of Orchids** at 2501 Old Lake Wilson Road houses the first permanent indoor display of orchids in the world, in a conservatory measuring 29,000ft² (2700m²). Recreating the steamy heat of the tropics, the park holds

---

### HORSE RACING

Ocala gained acclaim as a centre for horse racing when a locally bred horse called Needles was the surprise winner of the **Kentucky Derby**. Today there are some 400 horse farms in the area, many of which welcome visitors. To see the farms and enjoy the rolling hills and green countryside, drive southwest out of Ocala and down Route 200 towards Holder.
The largest racecourse in Florida is the **Gulfstream Park** track between Miami and Fort Lauderdale where the US$500,000 **Florida Derby** is run each March.

**CHURCH STREET STATION**

Once a mecca for all visitors to Orlando, the reviews are not as hot these days, though the new Club Paris – of Paris Hilton fame – is beginning to attract people back. The station was Orlando's first station and a major stop of the South Florida network. By the 1970s it was taken over and became an entertainment centre, packed with bars, restaurants and clubs. Then the theme parks became competitive. Still worth a visit if in downtown Orlando.

thousands of orchids in a variety of settings, hosts three orchid fairs a year and exports its product worldwide. Open Tuesday to Sunday 09:30–16:30.

The attractive Old Town shopping centre contains inviting, old-fashioned shops and restaurants, as well as a giant Ferris wheel and museums. The Old Town also offers weekly car cruises on Fridays and Saturdays, where visitors can see classic American and European cars, hot rods and muscle cars.

**Golfing** is a major attraction and many big-name designers have courses here – as well as some of the celebrity golfers including Greg Norman, Tom Watson, Arnold Palmer, Johnny Miller, Jack Nicklaus and Gary Koch. The **Ginn Reunion Resort** has just premiered its third course, the (6624m/7244yd) Tradition by Jack Nicklaus. The resort's other courses – the 6343m (6937yd) Legacy course and the 6636m (7257yd) Independence course – were designed by Arnold Palmer and Tom Watson respectively.

As in Orlando, most of the evening entertainment venues and restaurants here have climbed on the fantasy bandwagon. **Arabian Nights** (*see* At a Glance p. 61) brings exotic legends to life. At **Medieval Times**, visitors get to see knights, maidens, nobles, sword fights and jousting tournaments while feasting on hearty medieval fare. There is also a museum which offers a trip through a dungeon and shows by craftsmen in traditional costumes. The area's newest dinner attraction venue is **Tony 'n' Tina's Wedding**, where guests are cordially invited to celebrate an American-style wedding featuring the nuptials, followed by a rousing reception of a full Italian dinner, wedding cake, champagne and dancing to a live band.

**Below:** *While watching the show at Medieval Times, enjoy a wholesome meal – using only your hands.*

**Left:** *The dinner show at Arabian Nights offers Eastern delights such as belly dancing.*

## Polk County ★★

Like Lake County further north, Polk County, to the south, is a superb inland retreat, offering nature lovers over 600 **freshwater lakes**. Lining these tranquil lakes are the big, fragrant **citrus groves** and deep, dark **pine forests** that have helped to make the area a major scenic attraction.

This county, however, offers a pleasant mix of natural as well as cultural offerings. The **Black Hills Passion Play**, which depicts the last seven days of Christ's life, is held around Easter at the **Lake Wales Amphitheatre**. The big **Polk Museum of Art** is one of the largest museums in central Florida and the **Mulberry Phosphate Museum** houses some interesting displays of petrified dinosaur bones excavated in the surrounding region.

Among the places to visit is **Bok Tower Gardens**. This 128-acre (52ha) expanse provides a sanctuary for both fauna and flora. In the middle of the garden a 57-bell carillon tower chimes the hours, while musicians wander around and a varied programme of year-round concerts is sure to delight music lovers.

The **Fantasy of Flight** is an aviation-themed attraction that takes visitors back to early flight, World War I, World War II and beyond. Tour one of the largest private collections of aircraft in the world, experience a simulated battle mission over the South Pacific or cruise over central Florida in a hot air balloon.

---

### GOLFING FACTS

- 135 courses lie within a 45-minute drive of downtown Orlando.
- Nick Price, Lee Janzen, Ian Baker-Finch, Gary Player, Corey Pavin and Arnold Palmer are among the golfing stars to own a home here.
- Arnold Palmer, Jack Nicklaus, Tom Fazio, Robert Trent Jones, Greg Norman and Johnny Miller have all designed courses in the area.
- Walt Disney World® Resort has six courses within the complex.
- The World Cup of Golf was hosted by Lake Nona in 1993 and Grand Cypress in 1991.
- PGA tour events include the Walt Disney World®– Oldsmobile Classic, the Bay Hill Invitational and the Father/Son Golf Challenge. LPGA events include the Chrysler Tournament of Champions, the HealthSouth Classic and the Ginn Open at Ginn Reunion Resort in Kissimmee.

# Orlando and Central Florida at a Glance

The **summer** months, from June to October, are **hot** and humid with frequent short **thunderstorms**, but crowds are reduced, although the UK school summer holiday months of July and August are busier. The peak **winter** months are **December** to **February**, when Americans abandon the cold northeast and head for the winter sun. Parks are packed, but the weather is mild and drier, and so better for queuing.

**Orlando International Airport** receives scheduled air traffic while **Orlando Sanford** receives the international charter flights. Many European carriers fly direct; United States airlines have good domestic connections. Most hotels offer free **shuttles** from and to the airport. Public **buses** service the downtown area; there are also limousine and taxi services, both fairly expensive. Orlando and Kissimmee are on the **Florida Turnpike**, a toll-road from Miami and on **Interstate 4** which crosses the state from Tampa to Daytona Beach. Both 1–4 and **US192** pass the main access roads for Walt Disney World®. US 192 takes you near the main entrance of the Magic Kingdom®. **Amtrak** offers train services to Winter Park, and to Kissimmee.

**Driving** around Orlando is quite straightforward and 1–4

is the main artery. Plenty of **taxis** are available and a number of the attractions offer **shuttle** services from hotels. On International Drive, **I-Ride** shuttle buses operate a 15-minute service, running from 07:00–24:00. Children ride free of charge.

### Orlando
*LUXURY*
**Marriott's Orlando World Center**, 8701 World Center Dr, tel: (800) 621-0638, fax: (407) 238-8777, web: www. marriott.com Massive hotel with many facilities; attracts many convention delegates.
*MID-RANGE*
**Clarion Plaza**, 9700 International Dr, tel: (407) 352-9700. Next to the Convention Center, 1.2 miles (2km) from SeaWorld®.
**Las Palmas Hotel**, 6233 International Dr, tel: (407) 351-3900, fax: 352-5597. About 14 miles (20km) from downtown area, but close to the major attractions.
*BUDGET*
**Quality Inn Plaza**, 9000 International Dr, Orlando, tel: (407) 966-8585, web: www.qualityinn-orlando.com More than 1000 rooms, conveniently located.

### Disney
*LUXURY*
**Grand Floridian**, Lake Buena Vista, tel: (407) 824-2421, fax: (407) 824-3186, web: www.disney.ca/vacations/

disneyworld A grand hotel; very convenient for Disney with a monorail stop outside.
*MID-RANGE*
**Walt Disney World Dolphin**, 1500 Epcot® Resort Boulevard, tel: (407) 934-4000. Inside the Walt Disney complex. Massive Disney-style hotel.
*BUDGET*
**Disney's Pop Century Resort**, tel: (407) 938-4000, fax: (407) 938-4040. Part of Disney's wide world of sports complex and near the Animal Kingdom®.

### Kissimmee
*MID-RANGE*
**Quality Inn Maingate West**, 7785 W Highway–192, tel: (407) 396-1828, fax: 396-1305. Suitable for families; children's restaurant, pool and regular shuttles to Disney.

Orlando and Kissimmee have turned dinner theatres into a lucrative art form.

### Orlando
**Ran-Getsu of Tokyo**, 8400 International Dr, tel: (407) 345-0044. Japanese dining – reservations recommended, dinner only.
**Hard Rock Café Orlando**, City Walk, Universal Studios® Orlando, tel: (407) 892-7311, web: www.hardrock.com Guitar-shaped building with more than 500 items of rock 'n roll memorabilia to admire while eating.
**Christini's**, 7600 Dr Phillips Blvd, tel: (407) 345-8770,

# Orlando and Central Florida at a Glance

web: www.christinis.com
Upmarket northern Italian
cuisine; book ahead.
**Pirate's Dinner Adventure**,
6400 Carrier Dr, tel: (800)
866-2469.

*Disney World*
Restaurant information/reser-
vations tel: (407) 939-3463,
web: www.disneyworld.com
**Magic Kingdom**
Reservations recommended
for many of the main
restaurants, particularly the
character restaurants. But
there are also plenty of food
courts for fast food.
**The Liberty Tree Tavern**
Recreation of a colonial inn;
wholesome American food.
**Epcot**
Playhouse Disney's™ Play 'n
Dine at Hollywood & Vine,
Disney MGM Studios, sing,
dance and play with your
favourite characters from 'Jo Jo's
Circus' and 'The Little Einsteins'
at breakfast and lunch.

*Kissimmee*
**Arabian Nights**, 6225 W Irlo
Bronson Memorial Highway,
tel: (407) 239-9223. Dinner
show offering Eastern delights
such as belly dancing.
**Medieval Times Dinner and
Tournament**, 4510 W Irlo
Bronson Memorial Highway,
tel: (407) 396-1518. Toast
King Henry during a four-
course dinner with unlimited
beer, wine and soft drinks.
**Dolly Parton's Dixie
Stampede Dinner & Show**,
8251 Vineland Ave, Orlando,

tel: (866) 443-4943. Horses,
buffalo, singing and dancing.
**Tony 'n' Tina's Wedding,**
Pacino's Restaurant on 5795
US Hwy 192, tel: (866) 811-
4111. Celebrate an
American-style wedding, with
a full reception to follow.

**Orlando Mount Dora Village
Merchants**, Mount Dora, tel:
(352) 735-1191, fax: 383-
7524. Offering a look at a
quaint town with antiques,
boutiques and cuisine.
**The Florida Mall**, 8001 S.
Orange Blossom Tr, Orlando,
tel: (407) 851-6255, fax: 855-
1827. Unparalleled shopping
in Central Florida – fashion,
food and entertainment.
Features Burdines, Dillard's,
JC Penney, Parisian, Saks Fifth
Avenue, Sears, and more than
250 specialty shops.
**The Mall at Millenia**, 4200
Conroy Road, Orlando,
tel: (407) 363-3555. Good
shopping and restaurants.

**Bill's Airboat Adventure**, tel:
(407) 977-3214, web: www.
airboating.com Guided boat
tours on the St John's River on
board six-person airboats.
**Orange Blossom Balloons**, tel
(407) 239 7677, web: www.
orangeblossomballoons.com
champagne balloon flights at
sunrise, reservationa required.
**Boggy Creek Airboat and
Wildlife Safari Tours**, tel: (407)
344-9550. Guided boat tours
of Lake Tohopekaliga, private

and night tours. Guided wildlife
safari tours on a monster buggy.
**Walt Disney World**, **Sea-
World** and **Universal
Studios Orlando** offer **guided
tours**. Enquire at entrance.

**Central Florida Convention
and Visitors Bureau**, 1339
Helena Rd, Winter Haven,
tel: (863) 298-7565,
web: www.sunsational.org
**Orlando Official Visitor
Centre**, 8723 International
Dr, Suite 101, Orlando,
tel: (407) 363-5872, web:
www.orlandoinfo.com Open
08:00–19:00 daily for visitors
(except Christmas Day).
**Kissimmee Convention and
Visitors Bureau**, 1925 E Irlo
Bronson Memorial Highway,
Kissimmee, FL34744,
tel: (407) 847-5000,
web: www.floridakiss.com
**Lake County Convention &
Visitors Bureau**, 20763, US
Highway 27, Groveland,
FL34736, tel: (904) 429-3673,
web: www.lakecountryfl.com
**Walt Disney World Central
Reservation Office** (for in-
park accommodation), Suite
300, Lake Buena Vista,
32830, tel: (407) 934-7639.
**Walt Disney World Informa-
tion**, Box 10040, Lake Buena
Vista, FL32830,
tel: (407) 824-4321,
web: www.disneyworld.com
**Universal Orlando**, 1000
Universal Studios Plaza,
Orlando, tel: (407) 363-8000,
web: www.universal
orlando.com

# 4
# The East Coast

Speed is what this part of Florida is known for, from the deafening roar of rockets blasting into space to the burst of motor-sports action at the world-famous **Daytona International Speedway**. The region is also home to an extraordinary mix of beaches, parks, waterways and preserves that offer families plenty to see and do.

Halfway along lies the **Space Coast**, where the high technology of **Cape Canaveral** and **Titusville's Space Camp**, not to mention the **Astronaut Hall of Fame** (part of the Kennedy Space Center), rival for your attention. **Shuttle launches** take place throughout the year and should not be missed. The explosive blast-off of rocket engines contrasts strongly with the tranquillity of the nearby **National Wildlife Refuge** at Merritt Island and the parks surrounding DeLand.

The **Daytona Beach** area is well-known for its fabled 23-mile stretch of beaches. It is on the area's expansive shoreline that **Sir Malcolm Campbell** took Land Speed Records to a new dimension with his earth-shattering drive of 276mph (442kph) back in 1935. Modern speed addicts have to travel out west to the deserts of Nevada to find enough space to beat his times. Visitors can view Campbell's record-setting automobile the *Bluebird V*, along with a short film detailing his record attempts on the area's beaches, at DAYTONA USA – the official attraction of NASCAR.

Visitors to Florida's east coast should also take time to relax and enjoy the incredible natural beauty of long sandy beaches, dramatic Atlantic coastlines – and the lure of buried treasure. **Treasure Coast** to the south is named after the spilled contents of countless ships that floundered on

**Opposite:** *Rockets dwarf the visitors at Rocket Park, Kennedy Space Center.*

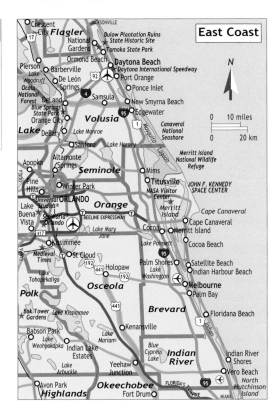

the sand bars well within sight of land. Experts claim that some 1800 Spanish galleons were wrecked on these shores more than 400 years ago and that their priceless cargo still remains, awaiting discovery.

Many golf courses and extensive water-sports facilities complete the picture of a superb outdoor area with plenty of distraction on offer for the entire family.

## VERO BEACH

At the centre of the Indian River citrus belt, the affluent resort of Vero Beach has a healthy mix of industries, but tourism is one of the faster growing. There are some 15 **golf courses** (not all are open to the public), numerous **boat charters** for fishing, canoeing and sailing and several well-maintained **tennis clubs**.

Museums in this city include the **Center for the Arts** on 3001 Riverside Park Drive, which mixes local, national and international exhibitions and is well known for its many seminars, concerts, workshops and festivals. The **McLarty Museum** situated on 13180 N Route, open 10:00–16:30 daily, concentrates mainly on Indian artefacts and recovered treasure and is dedicated to the hurricane of 1715 in which an entire fleet of treasure-laden Spanish galleons perished. The **Mel Fisher Treasure Museum**, at 1322 US1 in neighbouring Sebastian also houses artefacts salvaged from the numerous ships that floundered on this coast. The **Indian River Citrus Museum** takes a look at the industry behind the wealth of the region, while the **Historical Society** has an exhibition at the city railway station; both are located on 14th Avenue. **McKee Botanical Gardens**, on the east side of US1, was first opened in 1932 and its stock of plants is refurbished annually by the Indian River Land Trust.

The **Manatee Observation and Education Center** is a waterfront wildlife observation and nature education centre in downtown Fort Pierce. The Center lies just west of the Atlantic ocean and overlooks Indian River Lagoon, a saltwater estuary, and Moore's Creek, a freshwater creek and historical resting spot for the Florida manatee.

The camp site at **Sebastian Inlet State Recreation Area**, to the north of Vero Beach, is flanked by the Atlantic Ocean to the east and the Indian River to the west. Not only good for hiking and cycling, it also has snorkelling and scuba-diving opportunities – for certified divers only – and offers some of the best saltwater fishing on the east coast.

**Above:** *The citrus farming industry made Floridians wealthy at the turn of the century and still provides thousands of jobs.*
**Below:** *Golf has become big business – Florida has more golf courses than any other American state.*

**BEACHES**

Avoid the crowds and head out to the shores of Ormond By-The-Sea, Ponce Inlet, Klondike, Floridana, Canaveral National Seashore and Sebastian Inlet State Recreation Park. Or you can go for fun in the sun with the crowds at Cocoa, Satellite, Indian Harbor and Melbourne beaches. The best surfing is possible at Ponce Inlet, New Smyrna Beach, Cocoa and Playa-linda beaches or Sebastian Inlet.

## MELBOURNE

Continue north up Route 1 to find **Melbourne**, a turn-of-the-century city where the emphasis falls on history. The **Brevard Museum of Art and Science**, 1463 Highland Avenue, and the **Brevard Museum of History and Natural Science** in Cocoa both house visiting and permanent exhibitions and displays that tell the story of Florida from the Ice Age to the present. **Brevard Zoo**, 8225 N Wickham Road, has a Paws-On section to amuse children and adults alike and focuses on Latin American animals such as jaguars, llamas and monkeys. Open 10:00–17:00 daily.

At the **Space Coast stadium** you may be able to catch the Florida Marlin baseball team in training. This is also the place where you can enjoy many of the annual festivals which the city stages.

Just inland from Melbourne is **Palm Bay** and the **Turkey Creek Sanctuary**. A prime site for keen bird-watchers, this park is a major calling place for large flocks of **migratory birds**. Spring and autumn residents include rare woodpeckers and martins. **Manatees**, too, may be spotted from the 4000ft (1219m) boardwalk that takes visitors into the centre of the park and past some good bass fishing grounds. Call ahead on tel: (407) 952-3433 to find out when the park is open.

**Below:** *The Astronaut Memorial Planetarium and Observatory in Cocoa.*

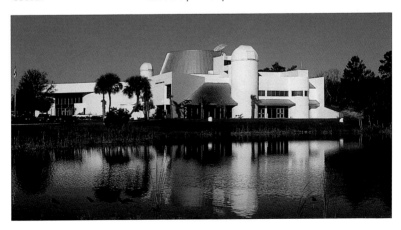

## THE SPACE COAST

The Space Coast runs for 72 miles (116km) north–south along Florida's east coast. Although this area is a hub of high-tech activity, it is also a great family destination, a sporting mecca and an eco-friendly environment.

North of Melbourne lies the city of Cocoa, the beginning of the Space Coast. Here you will find the **Astronaut Memorial Planetarium and Observatory**, where visitors can study images of the surface of Mars, look at the rings of Saturn, or watch comets smashing down on to far-off planets. Call tel: (407) 634-3732 for opening times. Shoppers will enjoy the restored **Old Cocoa Village** area with its brick pavements and cobbled streets.

**Above:** *The Ron Jon Surf Shop in Cocoa Beach has become a mecca for surfers.*

From Cocoa, cross over **Merritt Island** to reach **Cocoa Beach**, just south of Cape Canaveral. The Atlantic Ocean makes this a surfers' heaven and here you will find the famous (some would say infamous) **Ron Jon Surf Shop** – known by its outrageous billboards that line the coast. A must for shopaholics (even non-surfers will enjoy the spectacle), the shop is open 24 hours a day (web: www.ronjons.com). A neighbouring park is filled with sand sculptures and includes an 820ft (250m) pier that doubles as a grandstand for shuttle launch viewing; this is a popular spot for fishermen.

### Cape Canaveral

The **NASA Kennedy Space Center** covers 140,000 acres (56,000ha). At its visitor centre, the public can admire a 6.2 million-pound (2,811,179kg) replica of the shuttle *Explorer* and visit the **Astronaut's Memorial** honouring the memory of American astronauts who have died. Their names are engraved into a polished granite disk which rotates to mirror the sun's movements.

Exhibitions on the pre-Apollo Mercury and Gemini

---

### MAN IN SPACE

US President John F Kennedy sparked the space race in 1961. The Russians were ahead since one of their cosmonauts had already been in space, but Kennedy was determined: Americans would better them and send a man to the moon before the end of the decade. As a result, millions of dollars were pumped into **NASA**, culminating in the launch of **Apollo 11** and the historic moon landing in July 1969. The enormous cost incurred saw the industry going into decline until the launch of the reusable shuttle in 1981. This project, too, was initially fraught with problems. A fatal accident during the take-off of the **Challenger** mission in January 1986 caused a serious setback. The shuttle programme continues, albeit at a slower rate than the scientists would like.

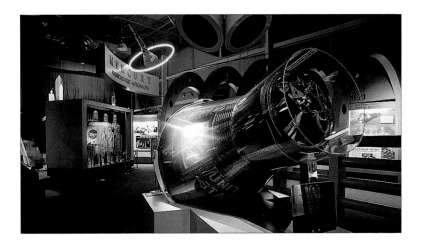

### TURTLE TALK

From May–Sep, Space Coast
beaches come alive as more
than 6000 loggerhead, green
and leatherback turtles arrive to
lay their eggs. The females lum-
ber ashore and dig nests. Each
of the 2000-lb (907kg) animals
will lay around 600 eggs (on
average, only one nestling will
make it to adulthood). After lay-
ing their eggs, the nests are cov-
ered, and the exhausted giants
make their way back to the sea.
Visitors can watch this night-
time activity on tours run by
the Sea Turtle Preservation
Society, tel: (407) 676-1701
from 12:00–15:00.
New Smyrna Beach's portion
of Canaveral National Seashore sponsors Turtle Walks
during nesting season.
Call 386-428-3384.
To learn more about sea
turtle rehabilitation visit Ponce
Inlet's Marine Science Center.

missions consume more of the visitor centre, as does the
**IMAX Theater** with dramatic space-related films such as
*The Dream is Alive*, including footage shot by astronauts
aboard the Space Shuttle, and *L5: First City in Space* – a 3D
exploration of the possible future colonisation of space.

The excellent bus tour allows visitors to spend as long
as they wish at three fixed stops. The **LC39 Observation
Gantry** brings views far across the space center and its
launch pads. The **Apollo/Saturn V Center** has countless
exhibits from the Apollo moon missions and a re-creation
of the first landing. Finally, the **International Space Station
Center** initiates visitors into the multi-nation project to
create a permanent orbiting space base.

Space shuttles still blast off from the complex regularly
and a provisional timetable is published every year.
Dates may change due to bad weather or for technical
reasons, but local tourist authorities are able to advise.
Alternatively you can call tel: (321) 499-4444 or visit:
www.kennedyspacecenter.com  Call 800-USA-1969 for
general information about the Space Coast.

### Titusville ★★

The most northerly city along this stretch of coastline,
Titusville boasts a late-19th-century Main Street, now

declared a **National Historic District**. It is also a vantage point for **shuttle launches**, and parking along the roadside is permitted up to 24 hours before take-off. Modern attractions include the **United States Astronaut Hall of Fame**, now part of the KSC Visitor Complex (KSCVC), which is operated by Delaware North Companies Parks and Resorts, and the **Valiant Air Command Warbird Museum**, which houses over 350 vintage aircraft, including Flying Tigers and C-47 Transporters, a Sopwith Camel and P-51 Mustang hardships. Flying displays are held annually in March. Open 09:00–17:00 daily, closed on public holidays.

**US Space Camp Florida**, open 09:00–17:00, allows children to experience the force of gravity and the thrill of aerial acrobatics. The **United States Space Walk of Fame**, filled with an abundance of memorabilia, lies alongside Indian River and overlooks the **Kennedy Space Center** – this is another favoured place for watching shuttle lift-offs.

**North Brevard Historical Museum** is worth a visit to see the handprints of the original Mercury astronauts, though nature lovers may prefer to explore the **Enchanted Forest**, a lush 400-acre (162ha) hardwood area with cabbage palms, saw palmettos, oaks and vines.

**Opposite:** *The Astronaut Hall of Fame in Titusville.*
**Below:** *Children meet a real 'moonwalker' at the Kennedy Space Center.*

Almost opposite Titusville on a spit of land which runs south from New Smyrna Beach to Cape Canaveral is Merritt Island, shared by NASA and the **Merritt Island National Wildlife Refuge**. One of the state's leading wildlife viewing areas, it adjoins the Canaveral National Seashore with its 24-mile (39km) beach. There are ranger-led **tours** of the reserve, observation towers for bird-watching and a visitor centre with information about the area. The refuge covers about 220 sq miles (572km$^2$), or 140,000 acres (56,657ha) and claims to provide a home for more endangered species than any other reserve in the United States. Manatees, bald eagles and loggerhead turtles can all be found here. Both Merritt and

### DAYTONA SPEEDWAY

Races are held from February to the end of October. The first is the **Sunbank 24**, a 24-hour race for sports cars. Trials start in mid-February for the **Daytona 500** stock car race – the classic of the year. By March it is the turn of the bikes, with half a million enthusiasts attending a **Bike Week Festival**. The **Pepsi 400** sees the cars back in July, followed by the **Daytona Pro-Am** in October. The **Bikoberfest** is the year's finale with races and shows.

Canaveral have boardwalks to take visitors through the dunes and shady hummocks (note that it is against the law to walk on the dunes). Surfing and beachcombing are particularly rewarding along this stretch of coast, though swimming is not recommended due to strong currents and the presence of stinging jellyfish. The best time for bird lovers to visit is winter, when huge flocks of migratory birds mill about.

### New Smyrna Beach ★

On the way north to Daytona Beach lies the quaint town of New Smyrna Beach. Founded in 1770, New Smyrna Beach was once the largest colony under British rule in the New World. It was developed by a number of enterprising Minorcan, Greek and Italian immigrants. The scenic **Spruce Creek Canoe Trail** starts and ends at Moody Bridge near New Smyrna Beach; its two loops leading through hardwood forests and salt marsh.

### THE DAYTONA BEACH AREA

The Daytona Beach area has been a family holiday destination for more than a century. The popular resort area which stretches from Ormond-By-The-Sea to Ponce Inlet continues to strive to be an all-around family destination. The **Marine Science Center** and **Ocean Walk Shoppes** – an oceanfront dining, shopping and entertainment complex – complement its growing list of family-friendly offerings.

Visitors can drive or park along 11 of the 23 miles (37km) of sands that helped **Sir Malcolm Campbell** into the record books. A fare is charged to obtain vehicle access to the beach. Vehicles are permitted to drive at just 10mph (16kph) – it is quicker by bicycle. Up to 500ft (152m) wide in places, the sandy beach is the focus of life in the city. Beach vendors sell everything from hot dogs to T-shirts and you can hire sunbeds and bicycles. Surfers head out

**Below:** *The New Smyrna Sugar Mill Ruins are a peaceful haven.*

early to catch the first waves of the day, while other water-sports enthusiasts may enjoy boating, para-sailing or jet-skiing. Deep-sea fishing charters are available in Ponce Inlet at the southernmost tip of the Daytona Beach area.

Spectators wander along the famous **Boardwalk**, which offers miniature golf, game arcades, fast-food outlets and shops. Equally attractive is the **Daytona Beach Pier**. Those wanting a really good view of the area should take a ride in the overhead gondola.

Shoppers should head to Daytona Beach's two weekly markets. The **Farmers Market** on City Island along **Riverfront Marketplace** – the city's historic downtown shopping dining and entertainment district – sells fresh fruit and seafood, caught or grown locally. Chefs from many of the town's 400 restaurants do their shopping here. Riverfront Marketplace is also home to a chocolate factory, gift shops, antique malls, restaurants, nightclubs, a chandler and an historical museum. The **Daytona Flea Market** presents 40 acres (17ha) of haggler's paradise. Everything from food to antiques is available here, including some real bargains as well as loads of tat.

The Daytona Beach area is home to several museums. The **Southeast Museum of Photography**, at 1200 W. International Speedway Blvd, Building 100, is Florida's only museum exclusively dedicated to photography. The 10,000ft² (930m²) museum is one of only 12 museums of its kind in the US and one of fewer than 30 in the world. SMP exhibitions have travelled to such respected institutions as the Metropolitan Museum of Art, The Carpenter Center at Harvard, and the Pitt-Rivers Museum at Oxford. Open Tue, Thu, Fri 10:00–16:00, Wed 11:00–19:00, Sat, Sun 13:00–17:00. Jun, Jul and Dec: Tue–Sun 13:00–17:00. Closed Mondays and the following times: Dec 24 to Jan 2 (Winter Recess), Daytona 500, Jul, Aug 1–13 (Summer Recess), and Thanksgiving Weekend.

**Above:** *Cars cruise along Daytona Beach, famous for its stock car and bike races.*

### PARTY TIME

**February** • Grant Seafood Festival, Melbourne: feast on oysters, clams and crabs.
**March** • Florida Marlins Spring Training, Melbourne: catch a pre-season game. Port Canaveral Seafood Festival, Titusville: fresh fish and gallons of chowder. Valiant Air Command Warbird Air Show, Titusville: a flying spectacular featuring Warplanes of all ages.
**Easter Weekend** • Easter Surfing Festival, Cocoa Beach.
**April** • Indian River Festival, Titusville: bikini contests, river raft races and celebrity look-alike competitions. Melbourne Art Festival: almost 300 artists gather to display local arts and crafts.

**Right:** *The watchtower on the promenade at Daytona Beach.*

### DAYTONA EVENTS

**Jan:** Winterfest; Native American Festival
**Feb:** Speedweeks (NASCAR)
**Mar:** Bike Week; Spring Wine & Food Festival; Spring Car Show & Swap Meet
**Jul:** Pepsi 400 (NASCAR night race); Florida International Festival (biennial)
**Aug:** Bill McCoy Music Festival
**Sep:** Fall Wine & Food Festival
**Oct:** Biketoberfest®
**Nov:** Halifax Art Festival; Turkey Run; Birthplace of Speed Celebration
**Dec:** Tree Lighting Ceremony

### TIME OUT

Sportsmen have plenty of choice on the Space Coast:
**Boating** • Airboat rides on St Johns River, powerboating, sailing, cruising, jet-skiing, canoeing and rafting.
**Golf** • More than 288 holes of golf on 16 public courses.
**Tennis** • More than 10 public tennis courts.
**Diving** • Scuba diving in the ocean and at inland caves and springs, as well as off-shore snorkelling.
**Fishing** • Deep-sea charters, off-pier sea fishing, and river fishing from boats and banks.
**Sky-diving** • Even parachuting is possible in this area.

The **Museum of Arts and Sciences** on 352 S. Nova Road is worth visiting for its amazing collection of Cuban art brought to the area by former Cuban president Fulgencio Batista, who had a holiday home in the area and bequeathed his collection to the museum. This is also the place to see the impressive skeleton of a prehistoric giant ground sloth measuring 13ft (4m), which was found in the area. Open 09:00–17:00 Monday to Saturday, open 11:00–17:00 Sunday.

The performing arts scene is alive and well in Daytona Beach. The city is the official American summer home of the **London Symphony Orchestra** (LSO). In fact, the LSO has performed intact more times in Daytona Beach than any other place in the world outside of London. Since 1966, the LSO has been the featured performer at Daytona Beach's **Florida International Festival** – a 17-day entertainment extravaganza that features a variety of world-renowned performance artists. The festival is held biennially in July. Daytona Beach is also home to **Seaside Music Theater**, an acclaimed professional theatre company that presents Broadway-calibre productions accompanied by a live orchestra. In addition, the **Daytona Beach Symphony Society** annually hosts a season of classical concerts featuring world-renowned guest conductors and symphony orchestras. In January, the society sponsors **Winterfest**, a classical music festival.

Great **golf** is another reason why worldwide visitors choose the Daytona Beach area for vacation getaways. This stretch of the Atlantic coast is lined with championship greens that are open to the public. Daytona Beach is home to the international headquarters of the Ladies' Professional Golf Association as well as courses designed by Jack Nicklaus, Rees Jones, Arthur Hills, Arnold Palmer, Gary Player, Lloyd Clifton and Bill Amick. With an average annual temperature of 21°C (70°F), the Daytona Beach area is the perfect spot for year-round golfing fun.

## Daytona Speedway ★★

**Henry Ford**, **Louis Chevrolet** and **Harvey Firestone** were responsible for establishing Daytona Beach's reputation. They holidayed in the resort at the turn of the century and soon realized that the compact white sands were perfect for car racing. The **Ormond Hotel** in Ormond Beach was the place to stay in those days and so it was the wide expanse of beach out front that became the racetrack. The first race, held in 1902 between R E Olds and Alexander Winton, resulted in a top speed of 57mph (91kph). By 1935 this had increased to the 276mph (442kph) achieved by **Sir Malcolm Campbell** in his aircraft-engined *Bluebird*. The lessons learned by the motor manufacturers down on the beach were later put to good use during World War II, when aircraft designers used the new technology to plan fighter aircraft engines.

Eventually the stock car racers moved south from Ormond Beach, down to a wide patch of sand near Ponce Inlet, attracting thousands of followers. The mass of spectators forced the racers off the sand, and by 1959 the **Daytona International Speedway** on 1801 W International Speedway Boulevard was opened. Stock car racing is still held every summer. The **Daytona 500** takes place in February; motorcycle meets are held each March and October; and go-cart racing happens after Christmas.

**DAYTONA USA**, an interactive motor-sports attraction located beside the speedway, is open 09:00–19:00 daily. At DAYTONA USA you have the

### MARY McLEOD BETHUNE

Born in 1875 to freed slave parents, Mary McLeod Bethune was a champion of civil rights as well as rights for women. A friend of former First Lady Eleanor Roosevelt, she served as a presidential adviser to Franklin D Roosevelt and founded the National Council of Negro Women. She also set up Florida's first school for black girls in 1904, with savings of US$1.50 and five pupils. Her white-framed, two-storey house remains filled with awards and mementoes of her life and now forms part of the Bethune–Cookman College campus which has grown up around the original school. Free admission to the public, tel: (386) 481-2122, for tours.

**Below:** *Ponce de León Lighthouse towers above its surroundings.*

chance to learn about the history of motor racing, design your very own dream stock car, take part in a pit stop and tour the track.

In addition to its many car and bike races, the Daytona International Speedway hosts a series of events to attract owners of vintage cars including **Daytona Turkey Run** each November and the Spring **Daytona Beach Car Show & Swap Meet** in March.

### Ponce Inlet ★

South of town lies Florida's tallest light station – **Ponce De León Inlet Lighthouse** in Ponce Inlet, a wonderful point from which you can view the entire Daytona Beach area. The 100-year-old building remained in use until 1970; since then it has been fully restored as a museum, complete with gift shop. You can also climb the tower in the company of historical re-enacters, complete with 1930s keepers' uniform, and it has just opened a 'World War II at the Lighthouse' and Radio Room exhibit. Ponce Inlet's **Marine Science Center** at 100 Lighthouse Drive, specializes in sea turtle and bird rehabilitation and features conservation, mangrove and whale exhibits. Open 10:00–16:00 Tue–Sat, 12:00–16:00 Sun.

**Below:** *A linesman waves the chequered flag at Daytona Speedway.*

### Ormond Beach

**The Casements** in the city of Ormond Beach, to the north of Daytona Beach, was once the home of multi-millionaire **John D Rockefeller**. His house has become a cultural centre and museum and is on the National Register of Historic Places. It provides the setting for a series of concerts, exhibitions and events, including the Native American Festival, the annual Casements Christmas Walk and the Birthplace of Speed Antique Car Show. The house also holds a large

collection of scouting memorabilia. Open 08:30–17:00 Mon–Fri.

**Tomoka State Park** was once the home of Timucua Indians. Today it is open for hiking and canoe trails along the Tomoka River; visitors can also book escorted boat tours.

North of Ormond Beach lies the **Bulow Plantation Ruins State Historic Site** with its 18th-century ruin of a sugar mill destroyed by Seminole Indians. The park has hiking trails, angling spots and a canoe trail through salt marshes, which leads past magnolia and oak trees.

**Above:** *Tranquil solitude at De León Springs State Recreation Area.*

## DELAND

From Ormond Beach head west down Route 40 to Barberville, where the **Pioneer Settlement for the Creative Arts** offers a 45-minute guided tour, open 09:00–16:00 Monday–Friday, 09:00–14:00 Saturday, 11:00–16:00 Sundays and closed on major holidays. The **De León Springs State Recreation Area** nearby, once hailed as a fountain of youth, has trails and good picnic and fishing spots.

South on US 15 is **DeLand**, home of the Stetson University and Gillespie Museum of Minerals (open 10:00–16:00 Tuesday–Friday). The DeLand Museum of Art is primarily dedicated to exhibiting Florida artists or work about the state.

DeLand is a short drive from the **Lake Woodruff National Wildlife Refuge**. Canoeists will enjoy the serene waterways, while hikers and cyclists can follow the extensive paths to small pools which attract wildfowl.

South of DeLand is the **Blue Springs State Park**. Manatee sightings here are virtually guaranteed – particularly in winter. This is also one of the better known inland scuba dive sites, and certified cave divers can explore the waters each spring; snorkelling is also permitted. Camping is available but it is often full, so book ahead.

South of the park is **DeBary**, a town founded by Belgian wine importer Frederick DeBary in the late 19th century.

### RARITIES

The Space Coast is home to more than 25 mammal species, 310 types of bird and 700 varieties of fish. Saltwater fish include snapper, flounder, sea trout, grouper, wahoo, sailfish and tuna. Bass, perch (crappie) and bluegill are found in the rivers.
The area also contains more federally endangered species than any other area of the United States. Loggerhead, green and leatherback turtles can be spotted, along with Florida manatees, eastern indigo snakes, gopher tortoises, American bald eagles, wood storks, scrub jays and peregrine falcons – all on the endangered list.

# The East Coast at a Glance

The **summer** months, June to October, are **hot** and **humid** but tempered by cooling sea breezes. Also, the further north you are in Florida, the less chance there is of hurricanes.

**Winter** is the **peak season** with warm, **balmy days** and less rain, but the crowds are worse, as countless North Americans flood south to escape the icy conditions back home. If there *is* a cold snap, temperatures in this area will drop to around 40°F (4°C), so pack a coat.

**Daytona Beach International Airport**, 700 Catalina Drive, is served by American, Continental and Delta airlines with a network of domestic services. Melbourne and Vero Beach regional airports serve the Space Coast, but most international travellers will fly direct to Orlando and drive east. Hotels operate **shuttle buses** from the airports and **taxis** are widely available. There are also some shuttle buses from Orlando airport to coastal resorts – check with tourist offices for latest details (*see* Useful Contacts).

Daytona and the Space Coast towns are strung along **Highway 1**, which runs inland from the beaches but is the most convenient access route. **Interstate 4** runs

from Tampa and Orlando direct to Daytona. All major **car rental** companies are represented in Daytona and along the Space Coast. Greyhound buses make two stops: in Daytona Beach and in Melbourne.

**Driving** around is very straightforward as all the towns are well signposted. It is a relatively short trip to Orlando and the theme parks (only about 45 minutes from the Space Coast). Travelling south to Fort Lauderdale or Miami is a longer journey of about three hours.

**Taxis** operate around the clock in towns and they usually have ranks at the major hotels.

Every town has its own **bus service**, and Daytona Beach has a trolley service, **Votran**, running along Atlantic Avenue to take visitors up and down the main strip.

Accommodation on the Space Coast is very much cheaper than in the Orlando area and prices can drop to an average of US$49 per night during the low season, which is from June to September.

### Vero Beach
*LUXURY*
**Disney's Vero Beach Resort**, tel: (407) 939-7540. The first Disney hotel at the coast.

*MID-RANGE*
**Sea Turtle Inn**, 835 Azalea Ln, Vera Beach, tel: (772) 234-0788, web: www.sea turtleinn.com A 20-room hotel with beach access.

### Melbourne
*LUXURY*
**Radisson Suite Hotel Oceanfront**, 3101 N Highway A1A, tel: (321) 773-9260, web: www.radisson.com/melbournefl Spacious suites with beachside balconies, microwave ovens and fridges.

### Cocoa Beach
*MID-RANGE*
**Holiday Inn Cocoa Beach Resort**, 1300 N Atlantic Ave, tel: (321) 783-2271, web: www.hicentralflorida.com On the beach, with a pool and free parking available.
**Cocoa Beach Oceanside Inn**, 1 Hendry Ave, tel: (321) 784-3126, web: www.cocoa beachoceansideinn.com Rooms have balconies with ocean views; observation deck for shuttle launch viewing.

### Daytona Beach
*LUXURY*
**Adam's Mark Daytona Beach**, 100 N Atlantic Ave, tel: (386) 254-8200, web: www.adamsmark.com/daytona Beachfront resort; 400 rooms overlooking the ocean, green lawns stretch to the sand.

# The East Coast at a Glance

**The Villa Bed & Breakfast**, tel (386) 248-2020, web: www.thevillabb.com One of the city's superior small lodging options with just 4 rooms and a beach-front location.

*MID-RANGE*

**Mayan Inn Beachfront**, 103 South Ocean Ave, tel: (386) 252-2378, web: www.BWMayanInn.com Complimentary breakfasts; great views over the ocean. **Treasure Island Inn**, 2025 S. Atlantic Ave, tel: (386) 255-8371, web: www.treasure islandinn.com On South Daytona beach, with 3 pools.

*BUDGET*

**Cardinal Motel**, 738 N Atlantic Avenue, Daytona Beach, tel: (386) 252-1035, fax: 257-3571, toll-free: 800 555-2819. Weekly and monthly accommodation rates are available. **Copacabana**, 1201 S. Atlantic Ave, tel: (386) 252-1452, web: www.realpages. com/copacabana Family owned and operated for five decades, heated pool and beach location.

**WHERE TO EAT**

The central East Coast has a wide variety of eateries to suit every budget. This area prides itself on its seafood. Annual festivals celebrate oyster catches, seafood and river fish.

*Vero Beach*
Try out the excellent seafood at **Ocean Grill**, 1050 Beachland Blvd, tel: (772) 231-5409 or Old Dixie Diner at 1436 Old Dixie Hwy, tel: (772) 562-9945.

*Cocoa Beach*
**Bernard's Surf**, 2 S Atlantic Ave, tel: (321) 783-2401. Excellent seafood, dinner only.

*Daytona Beach*
**Lighthouse Landing**, 4940 Peninsula Dr, tel: (386) 761-9271. A good spot to sip cocktails and watch the sun go down before enjoying the fresh seafood. **Cruisin Café**, 2 South Atlantic Avenue, tel: (386) 253-5522. A bar, restaurant and a car racing museum all in one.

**TOURS AND EXCURSIONS**

**Kennedy Space Center**, tel: (321) 449-4444, web: www. kennedyspacecenter.com

See launch pads, shuttle engines and space travel artefacts.
**Adventure Kayak of Cocoa Beach**, tel: (321) 480-8632. Tour the coastline and catch glimpses of dolphins and manatees.
**A Day Away Kayaking & Fitness**, tel: (321) 268-2655. Guided kayak tours on the Space Coast's diverse waterways; meals included. Kayak rentals. Outfitter service.

**USEFUL CONTACTS**

**Daytona Beach Area Convention and Visitors Bureau**, 126 E Orange Ave, Daytona Beach FL32114, tel: (386) 255-0415, web: www.daytonabeach.com
**Space Coast Visitors Center**, 3445 Cheney Hwy, Titusville, tel: (321) 269-9345, web: www.spacecoast visitorscenter.com
**Indian River County Chamber of Commerce**, Tourism Division, 1216 21st St, Vero Beach FL32960, tel: (772) 567 4391, web: www.indianriver chamber.com

| DAYTONA BEACH | J | F | M | A | M | J | J | A | S | O | N | D |
|---|---|---|---|---|---|---|---|---|---|---|---|---|
| AVERAGE TEMP. °F | 58 | 59 | 64 | 69 | 75 | 79 | 81 | 81 | 79 | 73 | 66 | 60 |
| AVERAGE TEMP. °C | 14 | 15 | 18 | 21 | 24 | 26 | 27 | 27 | 26 | 23 | 19 | 16 |
| HOURS OF SUN DAILY | 12 | 12 | 12 | 13 | 13 | 14 | 14 | 14 | 13 | 12 | 12 | 12 |
| RAINFALL in | 3 | 3 | 3 | 2 | 3 | 6 | 5 | 6 | 6 | 4 | 3 | 3 |
| RAINFALL mm | 76 | 76 | 76 | 51 | 76 | 152 | 127 | 152 | 152 | 102 | 76 | 76 |
| DAYS OF RAINFALL | 7 | 8 | 8 | 7 | 9 | 13 | 14 | 12 | 11 | 9 | 7 | 7 |

# 5
# The Northeast

An area of immense contrast, the beautiful Northeast region contains both the oldest and youngest of Florida. This was where the Spaniards first gained a strong foothold in the state, and also where the first skyscraper was completed in 1901.

**Jacksonville** is the business capital of the region and covers the largest area of any city in the United States. Divided by the **St Johns River**, the city is a mix of modern skyscrapers and historical sites. It is also home to the country's largest brewery and gourmands will enjoy the riverside restaurants and cafés that give Jacksonville such a rich cosmopolitan flavour.

To the north lies **Fernandina Beach**, one of the nation's oldest cities, while to the south lies **St Augustine** where the oldest schoolhouse vies for attention with the oldest shop, the oldest church and the oldest fort.

The Northeast has miles of sensational beaches and picturesque lakes and rivers. Its proximity to Georgia and the rest of the United States helped the area develop as a tourist destination back in the last century. Today, although many visitors drive on south, there is still plenty to stop for.

Wildlife abounds in the deep forests and wide lakes, and **St Augustine Alligator Farm** is one of the most popular attractions. The proud history of the area is brought to life with a series of colourful festivals and realistic re-enactments throughout the year, while the younger cities contain a wealth of cultural activity and a wide range of shopping opportunities.

### Don't Miss

**★★★ The Spanish Quarter, St Augustine:** restored to its former 17th-century glory.
**★★ The Riverwalk, Jacksonville:** shops and bars, many restaurants and street entertainment.
**★★ St Augustine Alligator Farm:** birds, monkeys and tortoises, as well as alligators.
**★★ Amelia Island beaches:** some of the very best in the Northeast, with high dunes.
**★★ Marjorie Kinnan Rawlings' house:** Cross Creek home of the Pulitzer prize-winning novelist.

**Opposite:** The 'Stars and Stripes' flies out in St Augustine.

## ST AUGUSTINE

With more than 60 different historic sites and attractions, St Augustine has plenty to offer. The city claims to be North America's oldest town although this title has, in the past, been disputed by Pensacola in northwest Florida. What is clear is that St Augustine is the oldest continuously inhabited town in the United States. It was first settled in 1565 by the Spanish and several of their original buildings can still be visited today. A host of annual festivals helps to retain its historical appeal and brings the old world back to life. To explore the historic zone in the centre of town, either take a horse-drawn carriage tour or, better still, venture forth on foot. A good place to start is at the old **City Gate** (top of **St George Street**). Not only is this close to the main visitor information centre, but it also adjoins the **Castillo de San Marcos National Monument**, built by the Spanish in 1672. The unique material they used was *coquina*, a soft limestone made from broken shells and coral. The fort is surrounded by a moat and comes complete with turrets and walls 16ft (5m) thick. Visit the garrison rooms and try to catch one of the artillery demonstrations that are held on the gun deck.

At Number 14 St George Street you will find the quaint **Oldest Wooden Schoolhouse**, built before the American Revolution out of cypress and red cedar wood. A little further down the road is the **Spanish Quarter**, a fully restored and functional historical village with craftspeople making candles, weaving or spinning. All the items made here are used to continue the upkeep of the Quarter.

### CLIMATE

Although **summer** temperatures reach an average high of 89°F (31°C) between **July** and **October**, winter months reflect the more northerly position of the region. Temperatures between **January** and **March** can fall to an average 47°F (8°C) and there is a danger of **frost**.

### St Augustine

(map)

JACKSONVILLE
Ripley's Believe It or Not!® Museum
San Marco Ave
Castillo Dr
Castillo de San Marcos National Monument
Old City Gate
Orange
Museum Theater
Oldest Wooden Schoolhouse
Saragossa
Spanish Quarter Museum
Cuna
San Sebastian
Ponce de Leon Blvd
Spanish
St George
Cordova
Sevilla
Hypolita
Charlotte
Avenida Menendez
Anastasia Island
Carrera
CASABLANCA INN
Ribera
Treasury
Valencia
Basilica Cathedral of St Augustine
Plaza de la Constitution
Bridge of Lions
Flagler College
Cathedral Pl.
CASA MONICA
Malaga
Zorayda Castle
Potter's Wax Museum
King
Lightner Museum
Oldest Store Museum
Bridge of Lions
Matanzas Bay
La Quinta
Cadiz
Bravo
Cedar
Granada
Avenida Menendez
De Soto
Marine
ALLIGATOR FARM
Ribera
Aviles
M.L. King
Bravo
Bridge
Washington
Cordova
St George
Charlotte
Oldest House

0  250 yd
0  250 m

N

At the point where St George Street and Cathedral Place meet, stands the lovely **Basilica Cathedral of St Augustine.** This has undergone various renovations and remodelling, particularly after a fire in 1887. It still houses parish records dating back to 1594, the oldest known written records in the United States.

The **Plaza de la Constitution** was the centre of the original settlement and today houses a monument to the Spanish constitution of 1812 and a statue of Juan Ponce de León, the first European to set foot in Florida, back in 1513. The **National Archaeological Park** on Magnolia Avenue commemorates his quest to find the Fountain of Eternal Youth (*see* p. 10).

Turn left off St George Street on to King Street and then right into Artillery Lane to find the **Oldest Store Museum**, displaying some 100,000 items that would have been sold at the turn of the century, such as lace-up corsets, medicine containing 90% alcohol(!) and red flannel underwear. The shop attendants all wear authentic costumes. A little further down the lane is the **Oldest House**, which, under the auspices of the local historical society, has been preserved to reflect the life of its various owners; each room's decor illustrating a different era of its occupation.

Back on King Street you'll find **Zorayda Castle**, a reproduction of Spain's Alhambra, with treasures from around the world. The **Lightner Museum**, a few doors along, occupies the former Hotel Alcazar and exhibits 19th-century collectibles. Antique music boxes are a speciality and the attendants happily give demos.

The **Mission of Nombre de Dios**, on San Marco Avenue, is believed to have been the site where America's first mass was celebrated.

**Above:** *The Oldest Wooden Schoolhouse dates back to British colonial times.*
**Opposite:** *Inside the quaint Oldest Store Museum.*

## ST AUGUSTINE ALTERNATIVES

**Potter's Wax Museum**, 17 King Street: contains 170 historical figures, a wax workshop and shop. **Ripley's Believe It or Not!®** at 19 San Marco Avenue: unusual museum filled with oddities from around the world, an amusing place to while away an hour or two. **St Augustine Alligator Farm**, 999 Anastasia Blvd: be sure to catch the alligator show when a keeper gets terrifyingly close to the jaws of the animals; the only place to house all 23 species of the world's crocodiles and alligators. Call ahead for show times on tel: (877) 966-7275. Open daily 09:00–17:00.

**Above:** *The modern sky-scrapers of Jacksonville overlook the St Johns River.*
**Opposite:** *Jacksonville is home to a large brewing industry.*

## JACKSONVILLE

Named after General Andrew Jackson back in 1822, this city began as a tiny town called Cowford nestling on the banks of the St Johns River. Today it spreads out over the largest area of any city in the United States, is one of the most vibrant and, although bypassed frequently on tours of the state, has plenty to offer. Some of the downtown area can be explored by water taxi and by a futuristic monorail, but you need a car to reach the other attractions. It's worth planning trips carefully to avoid spending the day criss-crossing the river.

The **north side** of the downtown area is home to the city's Convention Center and **River City Playhouse**, staging both adults' and children's theatre, as well as the Courthouse, City Hall and Chamber of Commerce.

The **Florida Theatre** on E Forsyth Street is considered the cultural heart of the city and stages more than 100 events annually. The **Cummer Museum of Art & Gardens**, on the northwest bank of the river on Riverside Avenue, houses a fine art gallery, displays of early Meissen porcelain and an art education centre. Open 10:00–16:00 Tue–Fri, noon–17:00 Sat, 14:00–17:00 Sun.

On Zoo Parkway and bordering the Trout River is the **Jacksonville Zoo & Gardens** (open 09:00–17:00 daily). It houses 700 animal species, many in enclosures that imitate their natural habitat as in the African veld section.

Only a short distance away is the **Anheuser–Busch Brewery** on Busch Drive, where visitors can join a conducted tour of the plant to learn more about the beer-making process.

Afterwards enjoy a brew in the sampling room of what is reputed to be the largest brewery in the United States. Open 09:00–16:00, Monday–Saturday.

### THE BEACHES

**St Augustine:** the start of more than 20 miles (30km) of beach running northwards. Extremely popular, particularly at weekends.
**Ponte Vedra:** million-dollar homes and golf courses line this stunning beach, the most southerly of the Jacksonville Beaches. Public access to the sand is limited but worth the hunt for crowd-free sunning and shell collecting.
**Jacksonville:** a mix of commuters who travel into the city and tourists wanting to enjoy the beach.
**Neptune:** very much quieter, mostly a residential area.
**Atlantic:** lively area hemmed by restaurants, bars and disco. Great surfing.

**Jacksonville Landing ★**
The Landing on Independent Drive is a collection of shops and restaurants, many of which overlook the river, and has entertainers performing in the fountain plaza. It can be reached by water taxi.

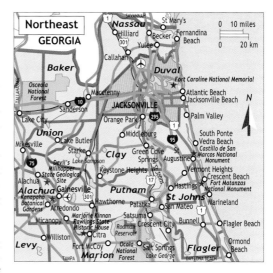

The **Riverwalk** on the North and South bank extends for some 1.2 miles (2km), has a fountain that is lit at night, a marina, water taxi station, restaurants, shops and street vendors. It leads to the **Jacksonville Museum of Science and History**, which incorporates an interactive Children's Museum. Call tel: (904) 396-7062 for opening times. The **Alexander Brest Museum**, on the campus of Jacksonville University, houses exhibits of Steuben glass, Boehm porcelain and pre-Columbian artefacts. The **Jacksonville Museum of Contemporary Art** on Laura Street features a permanent collection showcasing paintings, sculptures and photography created since 1945.

**Fort Caroline National Memorial** on 12713 Fort Caroline Road contains a model of the original fort. Open daily 09:00–17:00, closed Christmas.

## AMELIA ISLAND

The only part of the United States to have flown eight different flags, this 13-mile (21km) island has escaped much of the commercialism apparent elsewhere in Florida. The charming main town, Fernandina, was once the hotbed of pirates.

The **Museum of History** and **St Peter's Episcopal Church**, which served as a school for freed slaves, are worth a visit. Three miles (5km) north is the **Fort Clinch State Park** with a brick fort built by Americans to protect Georgia from further British intrusion after the 1812 war. The fort was only used during the 1847 Civil War when it was occupied by the Confederacy.

## DATES TO REMEMBER

**1562** French Huguenots establish a colony at Fort Caroline on St John's River.
**1565** Pedro Menéndez de Avilés founds St Augustine.
**1727** Oldest surviving house in St Augustine is built.
**1822** Town of Cowford is renamed Jacksonville after General Andrew Jackson.
**1832** William J Mills becomes first mayor of Jacksonville.
**1864** Florida's only major Civil War fight, the Battle of Olustee, takes place.
**1901** A huge fire destroys downtown Jacksonville.
**1908** Jacksonville starts to gain a reputation as the winter film capital with the opening of a major studio.

**Below:** *The entrance of the recently opened Harn Museum in Gainesville.*

## GAINESVILLE

Tourism officials around Gainesville call the area 'The Original Florida' because of its small towns filled with history, its bubbling springs and tiny fishing villages. Gainesville, the centre of the region, is the cultural capital of the area, home of the **University of Florida**. The campus houses the **Florida Museum of Natural History**, which contains fascinating displays taking you from dinosaurs to virtual reality. Open 10:00–17:00 Monday–Saturday, 13:00–17:00 Sunday.

The **Samuel P. Harn Museum** on Hull Road is one of Florida's latest institutions, exhibiting African, American and pre-Columbian artefacts across 62,000ft$^2$ (19,000m$^2$) of gallery space.

Be sure to visit beautiful **Kanapaha Botanical Gardens** on 63rd Boulevard. This is the second-largest garden in Florida and claims to be the most diverse.

In the downtown area indoor cultural activities take place at the **Center for the Performing Arts** which opened in 1992. Elsewhere, Constans Theater offers student productions that have been sponsored by the Florida Theater Department, while the Gainesville Community Theater puts on shows with other promising local talent. The Hippodrome State Theater by contrast, presents plays with international and national stars and is surrounded by pavement cafés, studios, bars and clubs.

South of Gainesville, down US441, the **Paynes Prairie State Preserve** is extremely popular with campers, hikers, horse-riders and canoeists. This area was once home to native Americans and artefacts found here date back to 7000BC. Some buffalo, horses and alligators are among the permanent residents.

A few miles away on Interstate 75 lies the Timucuan Indian village of **Micanopy**. The Spanish also made

**Left:** *Famous novels such as The Yearling were written on this typewriter, which can still be seen at the Marjorie Kinnan Rawlings State Historic Site.*

their home here, but little is left of anything predating 1821. Today the spot, which is filled with antique shops, is popular with film producers as an old world setting. Every autumn the village hosts a major antique market, attracting up to 200 dealers.

To the southeast is the **Marjorie Kinnan Rawlings State Historic Site**. The Pulitzer award-winning author of *The Yearling* made her home here in the 1920s and faithfully recorded the life she experienced around her in another novel, *Cross Creek*. Her typewriter still stands on the rather rickety porch, her letters and cuttings are on display, and a cupboard door stands ajar to reveal the place in which she hid her bottle of whisky during the Prohibition years. In March 2007, her home was formally dedicated as a National Historic Landmark. But be warned: only 10 people can enter the house at a time and there is often a queue, so bring a picnic for the wait, tour the gardens and visit the author's grave a few miles off at Island Grove. Open 10:00–16:00 daily. Note that house tours are not available August–September and are only available  Thursday to Sunday.

Travel north from Gainesville for 2 miles (3km) up the Millhopper Road to reach the **Devil's Millhopper State Geological Site**, a huge swallow-hole just over 120ft (35m) deep. At this marvellously picturesque site, streams tumble over the edge of a chasm amid surroundings of lush, exotic ferns and trees.

### CIVIL WAR BATTLE

Both sides claimed victory although the Union forces suffered more casualties and retreated after Florida's only Civil War battle which took place in the pine forests around Olustee, 13 miles (21km) east of Lake City and some 19 miles (30km) north of Gainesville. In February 1864 about 5000 Union troops moving east from Jacksonville confronted the same number of 'Rebels' for a five-hour battle that left some 300 dead and about 2000 wounded. The site is marked with a memorial and visitor centre. Once a year the forests come alive with soldiers as the battle is re-enacted.

## The Northeast at a Glance

The **Northeast** is much **cooler** than the Florida Keys, though temperatures rise dramatically in summer. Most **rain** falls in **summer**, but sea breezes keep the humidity down along the coast. From October to the end of March, temperatures drop and warmer clothes are needed.

**Jacksonville International Airport**, tel: (904) 741-2000, lies 10 miles (16km) north of the city and is accessible by bus or taxi. Road connections are good – **Highway 1** leads all the way down the east coast, from Jacksonville to Miami. **Interstate 95** comes through Jacksonville, and bypasses St Augustine before heading further south. To drive inland from Jacksonville, use **US90** which leads west to Tallahassee, crossing **Interstate 75** which heads south to Gainesville and Tampa. Rail connections in this part of Florida are poor. **Greyhound bus** services are good with north–south links and cross-country trips from Jacksonville, St Augustine and Gainesville.

Jacksonville's **water taxi** service sails up and down the St Johns River linking most of the major attractions on either shore and operating at 15-minute intervals.

Land-based taxis are easy to hire, though in Jacksonville water taxis are often much more useful. The local **bus** system is geared mainly for residents not tourists, and does not operate its full network late in the evening. All major **car rental** agencies have desks at the airport and in downtown Jacksonville. **St Augustine** is one of the few cities where tourists really ought to **walk** to take in the sights. The historic centre is compact and easy to navigate. If you have little time to spare, take a **trolley ride** or horse-drawn carriage tour. Boat and train tours are also available.

*St Augustine*
*LUXURY*
**Casa Monica Hotel**, 95 Cordova St, tel: (904) 827-1888, web: www. casamonica.com Located in downtown St Augustine it has 138 rooms, a private ocean-front beach club and outdoor heated pool and spa.

*MID-RANGE*
**Our House of St Augustine**, 7 Cincinnati Ave, tel: (904) 824-9204, web: www. ourhousestaugustine.com Intimate three-guestroom Victorian house with parking in St Augustine's Uptown San Marco Antiques District serves full gourmet breakfast. A short stroll to historic sights, shops and restaurants.

*BUDGET*
**Casablanca Inn**, 24 Avenida Menendez, 32084, tel: (904) 829-0928. Waterfront bed and breakfast establishment.

*Ponte Vedra*
*LUXURY*
**Sawgrass Marriott Resort**, 1000 PGA Blvd, tel: (904) 285-7777, web: www. sawgrassmarriott.com Luxury golf and tennis resort.

*Jacksonville*
*LUXURY*
**Quality Suites Oceanfront**, 11 N 1st St, Jacksonville Beach, tel: (904) 435-3535, web: www.jaxqualitysuites. com In the heart of Jacksonville Beach, an all suite hotel with spectacular views across the ocean.

*MID-RANGE*
**The House on Cherry Street**, 1844 Cherry Street, tel: (904) 384-1999, fax: 384-5013. Characterful, usefully-placed bed and breakfast inn.

*BUDGET*
**La Quinta Inn**, 8255 Dix Ellis Trl, tel: (904) 731-9940, web: www.laquinta.com

*Amelia Island*
*LUXURY*
**Amelia Island Plantation**, 6800 First Coast Highway, tel: (904) 261-6161, web: www.aipfl. com Offers a golf course and hiking trails through 1300 acres (526ha) of grounds.

## The Northeast at a Glance

*MID-RANGE*
**Elizabeth Pointe Lodge**,
98 S Fletcher, tel: (904)
277-4851. Bed and
breakfast establishment
situated on the beach.

*BUDGET*
**Hoyt House**, 804 Atlantic
Avenue, 32034, tel: (904)
277-4300. Bed and breakfast
with only nine rooms.

*Gainesville*
*MID-RANGE*
**Hilton University of
Florida Conference Center**
Gainesville, 1714 SW 34th St,
tel: (352) 371-3600, web:
www.hilton.com Good loca-
tion for access to the
university, big conference
hotel.
**Magnolia Plantation B&B
Inn**, 309 SE 7th St, tel: (352)
375-6653, web: www.
magnoliabnb.com Open
fires, jacuzzis and good
service are all part of the
package.

### WHERE TO EAT

*St Augustine*
**Columbia Restaurant**, 98
St George St, tel (904) 824-
3341. Good value Spanish/
Cuban cuisine, open year
round and children welcome.

*Jacksonville*
**River City Brewing Company**,
835 Museum Circle, tel:
(904) 398-2299. Wholesome
American fare, but often
visited simply for the micro-

brewed beers.
**Wine Cellar**, 1314 Prudential
Dr, tel: (904) 398-8989.
Elegant and pricey but
exceptionally good food.
**b.b.'s**, 1019 Hendricks Ave,
tel: (904) 306-0100. Typical
American fare for lunch
and dinner.
**Fatty Tuna**, 1173 Edgewood
Ave, tel: (904) 384-9669.
Japanese lunch and dinner
at affordable prices.

*Amelia Island*
**The Palace Saloon**, 117
Center St, tel: (904) 261-6320.
A colourful and atmospheric
watering hole with links to
Amelia Island's pirate past.
**The Surf Restaurant & Bar**,
3199 South Fletcher Ave,
tel: (904) 261-5711. Local
seafood with large outdoor
deck.

### TOURS AND EXCURSIONS

**St Augustine Scenic Cruise**, St
Augustine Municipal Marina,
tel: (904) 824-1806.
Interesting 75-minute cruises
along the city waterfront and
Matanzas Bay.
**St Augustine Sightseeing
Trains**, 170 San Marco Ave,

tel: (904) 829-6545.
A 7-mile (12km) tour past
no less than 80 points of
interest. Passengers may get
off at any of the 19 stops.
**Budweiser Brewery Tour
& Gift Shop**, 111 Busch
Dr Jacksonville, tel: (904)
696-8373. Informative
tours of the brewery and
beer tasting.

### USEFUL CONTACTS

**St Augustine–St Johns
County Chamber of
Commerce**, 1 Riberia St,
FL32084, tel: (904) 829-
1711, web: www.
getaway4florida.com
**Jacksonville and the
Beaches Convention and
Visitors Bureau**, 550 Water
St, tel: (904) 798-9111, web:
www.visitjacksonville.com
**Amelia Island Tourist
Development Council**,
961687 Gateway Blvd,
tel: (904) 277-0717, web:
www.ameliaisland.org
**Gainesville/Alachua County
Visitors and Convention
Bureau**, 30 E University Ave,
Gainesville,
tel: (352) 374-5231, web:
www.visitgainesville.net

| JACKSONVILLE | J | F | M | A | M | J | J | A | S | O | N | D |
|---|---|---|---|---|---|---|---|---|---|---|---|---|
| AVERAGE TEMP. °F | 53 | 55 | 61 | 68 | 74 | 79 | 81 | 81 | 78 | 69 | 61 | 55 |
| AVERAGE TEMP. °C | 12 | 13 | 16 | 20 | 23 | 27 | 27 | 27 | 26 | 22 | 16 | 13 |
| HOURS OF SUN DAILY | 12 | 13 | 13 | 13 | 13 | 14 | 14 | 14 | 13 | 12 | 12 | 12 |
| RAINFALL in | 3 | 3.5 | 3.5 | 3.5 | 5 | 5 | 6.5 | 7 | 7 | 3 | 2 | 2.5 |
| RAINFALL mm | 76 | 89 | 89 | 89 | 127 | 127 | 142 | 179 | 179 | 76 | 51 | 63 |
| DAYS OF RAINFALL | 8 | 9 | 9 | 9 | 11 | 11 | 12 | 13 | 13 | 8 | 7 | 8 |

# 6
# The Northwest

The Northwest, or **Panhandle** as it is often called, is bordered by Alabama to the north and Georgia to the northeast. This area is also known as the **Emerald Coast** after the vivid greens and rich blues of the sea that contrast starkly with its white beaches.

The Northwest has had a totally different development pattern from the rest of the state. The first area to be won over by the Americans, it was also the most closely involved in the Civil War. Industry and agriculture have been linked to northern neighbouring states rather than the citrus belt to the south.

Early settlers tried their luck in **Pensacola**, but a combination of disease and hurricanes forced them out and it was St Augustine that became the first established colony in Florida. The two cities have since argued fiercely over which is the oldest settlement in the United States, which led to **Tallahassee** becoming state capital as a compromise. Tallahassee is closer to Atlanta than to Miami, and magnolias and live oaks rather than palm trees colour the scenery.

Beyond the historic towns, the region is studded with springs, forest reserves, tunnels, caves and coastal parks, including the **Florida Caverns State Park** with its intriguing calcite formations. Other interesting parks include the **Natural Bridge Battlefield State Historic Site**, where Confederate soldiers once battled to save Tallahassee from falling into enemy hands, and the **Torreya State Park** with its 150ft (46m) bluffs towering high above the Apalachicola River. (Website: www.floridastateparks.org)

## DON'T MISS

**\*\*\* Cedar Key:** a tranquil reminder of times gone by.
**\*\* North Hill Preservation District:** dating back to Pensacola's origins.
**\*\* Panama City Beach:** a 27-mile (43km) stretch of dazzling, fine white sand beach considered one of the best in the world.
**\*\* 22nd floor of the New Capitol, Tallahassee:** a fine view of the capital city.
**\*\* National Museum of Naval Aviation:** one of the world's largest aircraft museums.

**Opposite:** *One of the many spectacular sunsets on the northwestern Panhandle.*

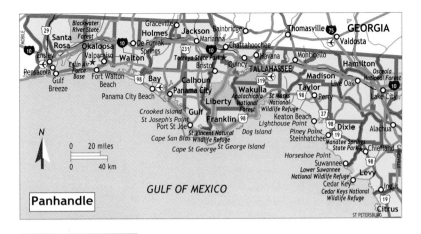

**Panhandle**

*GULF OF MEXICO*

The **summer** months of **July** and **August** are **hottest** with temperatures reaching an average of 92°F (33°C). The spring months from April to June can average a chillier 63°F (17°C), while winter temperatures can fall to an average 44°F (7°C) between January and March. **Hurricanes** hit this coastline after travelling across the Gulf – they are most likely in **August** and **September**.

## PENSACOLA

First inhabited in 1559 by a group of Spanish settlers headed by Don Tristan De Luna, Pensacola is extremely proud of its history and the fact that it has been ruled by five nations. The Spanish, after abandoning their original settlement, returned in 1698 to build a fort at the site of the present day Naval Air Station. Subsequently, control of the city shifted uneasily between the Spanish and British, until it became part of the United States in 1821 with General Andrew Jackson as its first governor.

The **Civil War** divided the city, with Southerners holding Fort McRee and the Yankees holed up in Fort Pickens on the offshore island of Santa Rosa (today's Pensacola Beach, which is the site of most of the resort hotels). The 'rebels' finally fled and Pensacola was taken for the North. In 1886, little **Fort Pickens** became the city's first real tourist destination as eager crowds flocked to catch a glimpse of the prominent and feared Apache chief, **Geronimo**.

## Seville, Palafox and North Hill ★★

Starting at the west end of **Three Mile Bridge** you first reach the historic district of **Seville**. Once the centre of the Spanish town, it is now a mix of Creole (some dating from the 1780s) and Victorian homes – many of which have been restored and converted into shops or restaurants. The centre of this area, **Seville Square**, is surrounded by live oaks and provides the setting for the annual Greater Gulfcoast Arts Festival, held on the first weekend of November, which attracts in excess of 100,000 people (www.ggaf.org), as well as the Jazz- or Springfest, a three-day event in April. Off to one side is Alcaniz Street with St Michael's Cemetery containing several thousand graves, some over 200 years old.

To the west lies **Palafox Historic District**. Wrought iron balconies grace Spanish architecture in what was once the commercial district of old Pensacola. Walking on, you reach **North Hill Preservation District**, an upper-class neighbourhood from the 1870s with examples of Queen Anne, neoclassical, Mediterranean and Tudor Revival architecture. It was built on the site of an old fortress, and people still find cannonballs in their gardens.

South of North Hill lies **Historic Pensacola Village** (open 10:00–16:00 Monday–Saturday; closed on state holidays), commemorating the city's past 200 years in a series of exhibitions. The **Museum of Industry** concentrates on the economic past, while old **Christ Church** houses the Pensacola Historical Museum. Other sites include the Julee Cottage Museum of Black History, Lavalle House and Quina House. The **Pensacola Museum of Art** on Jefferson Street once served as a prison. Further down the street, the old city hall has become the **TT Wentworth Jr Florida State Museum** and now houses a very interesting Kidstown display on the second floor, guaranteed to delight children of all ages.

**Opposite:** *Many of Pensacola's houses date back to the 1780s.*
**Below:** *The National Museum of Naval Aviation in Pensacola.*

## ALONG THE COAST

The past few years has seen development of the resorts along the coast between Pensacola and Panama City, Fort Walton and Destin, in particular, have enjoyed growth with large resort complexes opening on the spectacular beaches that make up the Emerald Coast.

## PANAMA CITY BEACH

Citizens of Panama City Beach are proud of their magnificently white soft beach, and with good reason. In 1994 the stretch of beach at St Andrews State Park was declared the best in America by the University of Maryland's laboratory for coastal research. The young crowd agrees, and each spring some 500,000 American students descend for their traditional spring break. Made legendary by Hollywood, spring breaks are known for riotous behaviour and some Florida cities have been eager to persuade the students to move on. Panama City Beach, however, extends a warm welcome while encouraging consideration for other visitors. Panama City Beach is also a favourite with families because of its lower costs, excellent facilities and more than 300 days of sunshine per annum, as well as a growing reputation for tasty seafood dishes.

### Local Attractions ★★

The area is divided by St Andrews Bay with Panama City lying to the east and Panama City Beach 5 miles (8km) west. Most visitor attractions are on the beach.

**Left:** *Interesting exhibits at the Museum of Man in the Sea, Panama City.*
**Opposite:** *Fort Walton Beach, one of many stunning white beaches along the Emerald Coast.*
**Below:** *The Emerald Coast is great sailing territory.*

**Gulf World** on 15412 Front Beach Road has four shows daily featuring dolphins, penguins and sea lions. There is also a tropical garden, scuba diving and shark feeding demonstrations. The park opens at 09:00 daily. Call tel: (850) 234-5271 for more information. **Coconut Creek Family Fun Park** is also on Front Beach Road, tel: (850) 234 2625.

Another attraction is the **Bay County's Junior Museum** on 1731 Jenks Avenue, where children can play Indian games and explore a tepee, log cabin and a pioneer village, as well as a nature trail. Open Mon–Fri 09:00–16:30, Sat 10:00–16:00, closed Sun and major holidays.

The **Visual Art Center of Northwest Florida** is on E Fourth Street. Exhibits change every six weeks and visitors are encouraged to join classes or workshops.

The award-winning **St Andrews State Park** at the southeastern tip of Panama City Beach, covers 1260 acres (510ha). It has two fishing piers, water-sports facilities and picnic sites, and its beaches are a paradise for beach-combers; there are also camping facilities.

### TALLAHASSEE

Billed as 'Florida with a Southern accent', Tallahassee is a town of historic homes set amid plantations and magnolia trees, bustling with politics and commerce. It also makes a good base for exploring nearby scenic attractions and soaking up the plentiful history and culture of the area.

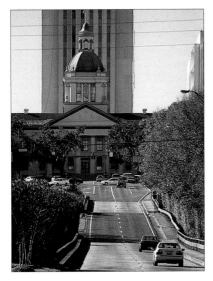

## City Hall, the Old and the New Capitol ★

The **Old Capitol** is situated on the corner of the Apalachee Parkway and S Monroe Street and was opened in 1845 when the city was declared the state capital. Altered in 1902, the stately building has retained its magnificent stained-glass dome, as well as the impressive rotunda and political chambers. It takes about 45 minutes to view all the exhibits inside, outlining Florida's history and political evolution. The **New Capitol** comes alive during the political session (March–May). The 22nd floor offers a panoramic view of the city and on clear days you can see as far as the Gulf of Mexico. Self-guided tours are available during regular New Capitol hours, 08:00–17:00 weekdays, closed weekends. Free guided group tours may be booked in advance by calling (8500 488-6167. The Visitors Info Center on the plaza level is open 08:00–17:00 weekdays, closed weekends.

Near the New Capitol, two blocks west on S Bronough Street, is the **Museum of Florida History** where recovered Spanish treasure vies for attention with prehistoric finds. War relics and a steamboat complete the collection. Open 09:00–16:30 Monday–Friday; 10:00–16:30

**Above:** *The new towers above the Old Capitol building in Tallahassee.*
**Opposite:** *The fine façade of the Supreme Court.*

### TALLAHASSEE FACTS

*Tallahassee* is the Apalachee Native American word for 'old town' or 'land of old fields', and today supports a population of 150,624.
It lies in the eastern time zone and, like Rome, is surrounded by seven hills. The only uncaptured Confederate capital east of the Mississippi, the city preserves the site of the Battle of Natural Bridge.

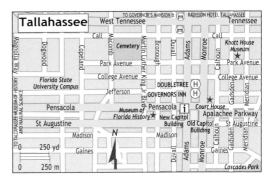

Saturday; 12.00–16:30 Sunday and holidays. For more information check www.flheritage.com

Further north on neighbouring N Adams Street is the Georgian-style **Governor's Mansion**. Its state rooms are filled with fine antiques and gifts from abroad. Only five rooms are open to the public, tours of which are available during legislative session and Christmas holidays. Call tel: (850) 488-4661 for times.

## Museums and Archaeological Sites ★

Head out of the downtown area on E Park Avenue to the **Knott House Museum**, built by a free Black builder in 1843, which today houses a large collection of gilt-framed mirrors. Rhymes written on silk ribbons by its eccentric owner are attached to the furniture. This was the site of the formal declaration of emancipation of North Florida slaves in 1865, officially freeing all remaining slaves in the state.

The city is an easy drive from America's greatest concentration of plantations – 71 estates scattered across Southern Georgia, close to Thomasville.

On a hill to the west of town near the intersection of Tennessee Street and W Mission Road lies **Mission San Luis**, the archaeological and historic site of the home of Apalachee Indians and Spanish settlers from 1656 to 1704.

**WALKABOUT**

Tallahassee has at least three easy walking routes to take in the main sights. Free walking maps are available at the **Tallahassee Area Visitor Information Center**, New Capitol Building.
**Downtown:** start from the New Capitol for a taste of the city as political and retail centre with varied architecture and shopping.
**Park Avenue Historic District Tour:** explore the city's historic churches, old cemetery and the parks which were once a dirt clearing to protect the city from attack.
**Calhoun Street Historic District Tour:** has the largest concentration of historic homes and was once known as Gold Dust Street, due to its many wealthy residents.

*Above: St Mark's light-house was built with stone from a 17th-century fort.*

An annual heritage festival includes costumed re-enactments and there are also regular excavations around the 50-acre (20ha) plot. Another historical re-enactment takes place at the **De Soto Archaeological Site** off Lafayette Street, the place where Hernando de Soto and his troops celebrated the first Christmas in America, back in 1539.

The **Tallahassee Museum of History and Natural Science** on Museum Drive has native red wolves, Florida panthers and alligators living on 52 acres (21ha) alongside an 1880s farm exhibit and a plantation home.

## State Parks ★★

Tallahassee is surrounded by numerous state parks, including the **Florida Caverns State Park** near Marianna, which provides hourly tours through caves and caverns filled with spectacular calcite formations: soda straws, stalactites, stalagmites, columns, flow-stones and draperies. Open 08:00–sunset daily. This is the only cavern, visitors can walk into as the rest are underwater caves.

The **Torreya State Park** is the site of Gregory House, a former cotton plantation; the surrounding park is filled with the rare torreya evergreen, as well as yew trees and the US champion-winged elm. Open 08:00–sunset daily, house tours 10:00 Monday–Friday, and 10:00, 14:00, 16:00 on Saturday and Sunday.

The **Apalachicola National Forest** includes more than 500,000 acres (202,347ha) of untouched native forest and lies just 10 miles (17km) south of the city. Tallahassee is also surrounded by lakes, among them Lake Jackson, Lake Bradford and Lake Talquin.

### SOUTH FROM TALLAHASSEE

A Spanish mission and 17th-century fort made **St Marks** a powerful place. Stones from the fort were used to build a lighthouse which is still in operation today. A later Civil War fort here was separately occupied by each of the opposing sides.

Once the third-largest cotton port on the Gulf Coast, nearby **Apalachicola** served as a base for blockade runners during the Civil War. It is now the state's most important oyster fishery – and home to the John Gorrie State Museum, dedicated to the man who invented fridges, ice-makers and air conditioners (see page 14). To the north and west is the **Apalachicola National Forest** and the **Torreya State Park**, named after the rare 'torreya' tree which is said to have grown in the garden of Eden.

## SOUTH TO CEDAR KEY

Fifty miles (80km) out of Tallahassee you reach the inland town of **Perry**, once famed for its logging production. The **Forest Capital State Museum** has an authentic 'Cracker' farm, a homestead typical of this area.

**Hickory Mound Impoundment** west of Perry offers canoeing, hiking and cycling trails. Call tel: (850) 838-1306 to check the hunting season dates, when the area is closed.

South of Perry the US98 runs down to Cedar Key. Stop off at **Keaton Beach** or **Steinhatchee** on the way; both with numerous bars and seafood restaurants overlooking the Gulf – excellent places to relax and watch the sun set.

A few miles south on US98, turn right down Highway 349 to reach the **Manatee Springs State Park**, where a spring spills out an average 116.9 million gallons (532 million litres) of water daily. Manatees can be spotted here, and water-sports enthusiasts are well catered for; there are also picnic areas.

The springs feed the **Suwannee River** which flows for more than 200 miles (322km) across Florida from the Okefenokee Swamp in Georgia. At the mouth of the river, the town of Suwannee is a good place to hire a houseboat for a few days, or take a boat trip into the Gulf for the day.

Along the stretch of coastline known as **Big Bend**, swamps, riverlets and islands take over. Charming **Cedar Key**, at the end of Route 24, lies on an island at the outer limit of the marshes. Once a thriving port, the village lost importance as ships grew too large for the shallow waters, but much of its shipping history – plus a fine shell collection – is displayed in the **Cedar Key State Museum**. Call tel: (904) 543-5350 for opening times. **Cedar Key Scrub State Reserve** provides 4000 acres (1619ha) of marsh habitat for seabirds, manatees, eagles, and even black bears.

### WAKULLA SPRINGS

*Wakulla* is a native American word meaning 'mysterious waters', an apt title for this wilderness area, 12 miles (19km) south of Tallahassee. Virtually untouched, the area was the setting for Tarzan movies in the 1930s. Today glass-bottom boats take visitors over the 'bottomless' springs which are said to be among the deepest in the world – it is still a mystery exactly how deep. Scuba divers can venture into the depths, while boat tours afford a glimpse of alligators, snakes and numerous birds – some 154 species have been spotted in the area.

**Below:** *Heed the warning signs at the Apalachicola National Forest.*

## The Northwest at a Glance

Unlike most of Florida, the Northwest experiences little seasonal fluctuation. With water temperatures around 70°F (21°C) and air temperatures of 74°F (23°C), the region is **pleasant** all **year-round**.

No direct flights from Europe service this area as yet, but the **regional airports** at Tallahassee, Pensacola, Fort Walton/Okaloosa County and Panama City receive connecting flights from the major United States carriers. **Taxis** and hotel **shuttle buses** are the main mode of transport from and to the airports. **Road** connections to the Northwest area are good. **Interstate 10** (I–10) runs east–west from Tallahassee to Pensacola. **Highway 85** goes south, from I–10 to Fort Walton Beach, which is also accessible from Pensacola, along **Highway 98**. Panama City is reached from I–10 south along **Highway 231**. **Train** connections are difficult, but **Greyhound buses** run to this coast from Alabama and from Georgia.

The major **car rental** companies have desks at the airports and in downtown locations. Local **buses** and shuttle buses run along the beach in Panama City Beach but only during daylight hours.

### Pensacola Beach
*LUXURY*
**Dunes**, 333 Ft Pickens Rd, tel: (850) 932-3536. On the beach, offers a putting green and golf packages.

*MID-RANGE*
**Five Flags Inn**, 299 Ft Pickens Rd, tel: (850) 932-3586. Facing the Gulf.

*BUDGET*
**Best Western Resort Pensacola Beach**, 16 Via De Luna Dr, toll-free: 800 934-3301.

### Panama City Beach
*LUXURY*
**Marriotts Bay Point Resort Village**, 4200 Marriott Dr, tel: (850) 236-6000. Spacious golf resort.

*MID-RANGE*
**Holiday Inn Sunspree Resort**, 1127 Front Beach Road, tel: (850) 234-1111. Good for families.

*BUDGET*
**Best Value Inn**, 15013 Front Beach Rd, tel: (850) 234-8845, web: www.pcbeachmotel. com Gulf front rooms and a range of facilities nearby.

### Tallahassee
*MID-RANGE*
**Park Plaza Hotel Tallahassee**, 415 N Monroe St, tel: (850) 224-6000, fax: 878-9964, ext. 4118. In downtown area.

**Governors Inn**, 209 S Adams St, tel: (850) 681-6855, web: www.thegovinn.com In the heart of the city, offering comfort and old-world luxury.

*BUDGET*
**Best Western**, 2016 Apalachee Parkway, tel: (850) 656-6312, toll-free: 800 827-7390. Within walking distance of the centre of town.

The long shoreline contributes to a love of seafood. Panacea claims to be the blue crab capital of the world and Apalachicola oysters are justifiably famous.

### Pensacola Beach
**Boy on a Dolphin**, 400 Pensacola Beach, tel: (850) 932-7954. Famous for fresh seafood and steaks.
**Flounder's Chowder & Ale House**, 800 Quietwater Beach Rd, tel: (850) 932-2003. Award-winning seafood, great desserts.
**Jubilee Restaurant**, 400 Quietwater Beach Rd, tel: (850) 934-3108. American cuisine, good for special occasions.

### Panama City Beach
**Boar's Head**, 17290 Front Beach Road, tel: (850) 234-6628. Best known for its prime rib; high prices but worth it.
**Capt. Anderson's Restaurant**, 5551 N Lagoon Dr, tel: (850) 234-2225. Excellent seafood, low prices.

**Hamilton's Restaurant & Lounge**, 5711 N Lagoon Dr, tel: (850) 234-1255. Another good option for well-priced seafood.

*Tallahassee*
**Andrew's**, 228 S Adams St, tel: 222-3444. Award-winner; American-Italian; reservations are advised.
**La Fiesta Mexican Restaurant**, 2329 Apalachee Pkwy, tel: (850) 656-3392. Up to $40 for dinner, Mexican cuisine.
**Mozaik**, 1410 Market St, tel: (850) 893-7668. Good New American food at reasonable prices.

### SHOPPING

*Tallahassee*
**Governor's Square**, 1500 Apalachee Parkway, tel: 671-INFO. Largest selection of speciality shops in the area.
**Village Commons**, 1400 Village Square Blvd, tel: (850) 413-9200. Upmarket speciality shops mixed with factory discount stores.
**Waldo's Antique Village**, 17805 NE US Hwy 301, tel: (352) 468-3111. Large mall filled with collectibles.
**Downtown Havana**, 12 miles (19km) north of Tallahassee in historic quarter of Havana. Art galleries, cafés and speciality shops.

*Destin*
**Silver Sands Factory Stores**, 10562 Emerald Coast Pkwy, tel: (850) 654-9771. Claims to

be one of the largest designer outlet centres in the US.

### TOURS AND EXCURSIONS

**Action on Blackwater Canoe Rental and Campground**, 6293 Hwy 4, tel: (850) 537-2997, web: www.actionon blackwater.com Spend half a day on the Blackwater River.
**Wild Florida Adventures**, tel: (352) 528-3984, web: www.wild-florida.com Kayak tours leave from various points to travel along the scenic Gulf Coast.
**Big Bend Charters**, tel: (352) 498-3703, web: www.big bendcharters.com Full service charter company with standard or custom fishing trips.

### USEFUL CONTACTS

**Emerald Coast Convention and Visitors Bureau**, 1540 Miracle Strip Pkwy, Fort Walton Beach, tel: (850) 651-7131, web: www.destin-fwb.com
**Pensacola Convention and Visitors Information Center**, 1401 E Gregory St, Pensacola, FL32501, tel: (850) 434-1234, web: www.relaxinpensacola.com
**Panama City Beach**

**Convention and Visitors Bureau**, 17001 Panama City Beach Pkwy, tel: (850) 234-6575, web: www.800pcbeach.com
**Tallahassee Area Convention and Visitors Bureau and Tallahassee Visitor Information Center**, 106 E Jefferson St, Tallahassee, tel: (850) 606-2305, web: www.visitTallahassee.com

*Diving*
**Diver's Den**, 3120 Thomas Dr, Panama City Beach, tel: (850) 234-8717.
**The Scuba Shop**, 348 Miracle Strip Parkway, Fort Walton Beach, tel: (850) 243-3373.

*Golf*
The Emerald coast alone has almost 1100 golf holes – and counting.
**Emerald Bay Golf Club**, 4001 Emerald Coast Parkway, Fort Walton Beach, tel: (850) 837-4455.
**Signal Hill Golf Course**, 9615 Thomas Dr, Panama City, tel: (850) 234-3218.
**The Moor Golf Club**, 3220 Avalon Blvd, Pensacola, tel: (850) 995-GOLF (4653).

| PENSACOLA | J | F | M | A | M | J | J | A | S | O | N | D |
|---|---|---|---|---|---|---|---|---|---|---|---|---|
| AVERAGE TEMP. °F | 53 | 55 | 60 | 67 | 74 | 80 | 81 | 81 | 78 | 70 | 60 | 54 |
| AVERAGE TEMP. °C | 12 | 13 | 16 | 20 | 23 | 27 | 27 | 27 | 26 | 21 | 16 | 12 |
| HOURS OF SUN DAILY | 12 | 13 | 12 | 13 | 13 | 14 | 14 | 14 | 13 | 12 | 12 | 12 |
| RAINFALL in | 4.5 | 4.5 | 5.5 | 4.5 | 3.5 | 5 | 7 | 7.5 | 6 | 4 | 4 | 4.5 |
| RAINFALL mm | 109 | 117 | 137 | 109 | 96 | 129 | 177 | 193 | 152 | 99 | 94 | 112 |
| DAYS OF RAINFALL | 9 | 9 | 10 | 10 | 9 | 11 | 12 | 13 | 12 | 9 | 9 | 8 |

# 7
# The West Coast

Hostile natives and insect-infested swamps once saw this area frequented only by buccaneers in search of a hide out. Florida's West Coast is relatively new territory for European visitors too, but beaches, resort areas, private islands and a wealth of culture have started attracting tourists.

What Flagler did for the east coast in terms of development, magnate **Henry Plant** achieved here on the West Coast. Many elegant Victorian homes in Tampa and along the coastal strip owe their origins to Plant, who brought the railroad and, with it, industry and wealth.

**Tampa** lies at the heart of the West Coast development, characterized by its industrial history, port and tourist attractions. Nearby ethnic enclaves add their own inimitable style to the region; a Czech community in Brooksville holds regular strudel bakes in an effort to retain the ways of their fatherland.

The **St Petersburg** area has stunning beaches and spectacular sunsets. A string of islands leads down to **Sarasota**, where classical music mixes with the razzmatazz of the circus. The West Coast even has its own **Venice** – criss-crossed with canals and home to the world's only clown college. Further down the coast wildlife replaces city glitz as the main attraction, with **Fort Myers** and **Naples** surrounded by national parks and the vast **Everglades**. Many Americans have bought homes in this area, making it as rich and exclusive as its east coast counterpart, Palm Beach. Visitors always receive a warm welcome, whether driving through or staying awhile.

## DON'T MISS

★★★ **Sunshine Skyway:** enjoy the views of the islands and Tampa Bay.
★★★ **Busch Gardens:** thrill of roller coasters tempered with wildlife and gardens.
★★★ **Ybor City:** Cuban life, history and entertainment.
★★ **Corkscrew Swamp Sanctuary:** a wilderness of 11,000 acres (4452ha), inhabited by alligators, bobcats and otters.
★★ **John and Mable Ringling complex:** amazing combination put together by this famous circus couple.

**Opposite:** *Fun in the sun at Tigertail Beach on Marco Island.*

## CLIMATE

Temperatures fluctuate between summer and winter, with July to October basking in heat of more than 91°F (33°C), and winter lows of 54°F (12°C) between January and March. **Humidity** is high in **summer** and bugs abound. **Winters** are much drier and more **temperate**.

## TAMPA BAY AND SURROUNDS
### Tampa ★

Native Americans first discovered the natural attractions of Tampa, its harbour protected by the sandbanks of St Petersburg. **Hernando de Soto** was the first European known to have set foot here (1539) – in search of gold; the area remained largely undeveloped for the next 200 years. First called Fort Brooke, the town became Tampa in 1855, named after the Indian word for 'sticks of fire'. Thirty years later, **Don Vicente Martinez Ybor** moved his cigar factory from Key West to Tampa, not only building a world-renowned industry here, but also forming the base of the city's thriving Hispanic community. Cubans followed the cigar maker in droves but the rising popularity of cigarettes brought a stop to an industry employing some 12,000 people. Today **Ybor City** remains one of the most vibrant areas of Tampa with excellent restaurants and lively nightlife as well as colourful markets.

The heart of the beautifully restored Ybor City is the former cigar factory, **Ybor Square**, which is now an attractive shopping mall with many speciality stores, antique shops and ethnic restaurants. The **Old Hyde Park Village** is another restored section of the city, and is filled with upmarket shops, pavement cafés and chic restaurants.

West Coast

**Left:** *Spanish and Cuban restaurants are a must in downtown Ybor City.*
**Below:** *Riding the Python at Busch Gardens is only for the brave.*

The skyscraper area downtown is home to the **Tampa Museum of Art** on N Ashley Drive. Seven galleries house Greek and Roman antiquities along with some of the finest exhibitions in the state. Dedicated to **African–American art**, the museum on N Marion Street was the first of its kind in Florida and is famed for its Barnett–Aden collection.

Children may prefer the **Museum of Science and Industry** (MOSI) on 4801 E Fowler Avenue. The planetarium, space simulators and hurricane chamber are both educational and fun. There's also the Butterfly Encounter (walk-through cages filled with butterflies) and an Omni Theater with a 360° revolving dome. Open 09:00–16:30 Sunday–Thursday in autumn and winter, 09:00–18:00 Sunday–Thursday and 09:00–21:00 Friday–Saturday in spring and summer.

Tampa has its share of theme parks, from **Adventure Island**, offering speed slides and other water attractions, to **Buccaneer Bay** with yet more sensational water rides in a natural spring setting.

The **Florida Aquarium** at Garrison Seaport Center covers 152,000ft$^2$ (14,121m$^2$) and houses 4350 species of fish, animal and plant, while **Lowry Park Zoo** on 7530 N Boulevard has a manatee treatment tank that doubles as an emergency rescue clinic.

## The Pinellas Peninsula ★★

A fist of land separating Tampa Bay from the Gulf of Mexico, the Pinellas Peninsula is largely consumed by uninteresting suburbia. However, the splendid coastline is fringed by a 28-mile (45km) string of barrier islands, locally called the Pinellas Suncoast, connected by road to the mainland and to each other by Gulf Boulevard. Adding to the obvious appeal of the beaches is the area's reputation for sunshine: 768 consecutive sunny days were recorded in the 1960s. Away from the coast you will find the Pinellas Peninsula's only place of merit, the city of St Petersburg.

## St Petersburg ★★

Once nationally-known as a retirement community, St Petersburg has enjoyed an influx of younger settlers and developed into a surprisingly vibrant and enjoyable place where most things of interest are within walking distance of one another. One major addition has been the **Florida International Museum** which turned a former department store into a vast exhibition space for major travelling shows. These have ranged from the treasures of the Russian Tsars to items recovered from the Titanic. Such is the museum's popularity, that bookings often have to be made in advance. Phone (727) 341-7900 for the latest exhibition and booking details.

A longer established but not less remarkable cultural offering is a major collection of works by the surrealist artist Salvador Dali. The **Salvador Dali Museum** was established by a wealthy American couple who befriended the artist on his first trip to the US in the 1930s and subsequently purchased many of his works. The museum is arranged to give a chronological view

**Below:** *Fabulous St Pete Beach, a good place to be on a hot day.*

of Dali's work, from early orthodox paintings to the gigantic canvases mostly created during the 1950s and '60s.

The **Pier** has become a central point in the newly refurbished downtown area, with a constant stream of events, day and night. There are events for the golden oldies, families, music and theatre to name but a few.

**The Pinellas Beaches** can be accessed by several routes across the peninsula. The most dramatic first impression, though, is found on the approach from St Petersburg on Route 682, with the bright pink profile of the **Don CeSar Hotel**, a luxury resort, rising on the beach.

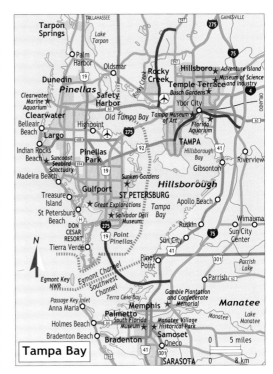

Tampa Bay

Built in the 1920s, the Don CeSar (guided historical tours are available; tel: (727) 360 1881) marks the southern end of **St Pete Beach**, one of the biggest and busiest of the coastal communities. If time permits, head south into Pass-a-Grille, a village-like settlement with few trappings of tourism despite its excellent beaches and the enjoyably ramshackle **Gulf Beaches Historical Museum** on Tenth Avenue. Passing through St Pete Beach, the outlook of motels, restaurants and shopping plazas, and glimpses of uniformly excellent beaches, is one that continues for miles northwards on Gulf Boulevard. Worthwhile stops include Madeira Beach's **John's Pass Village** and the **Suncoast Seabird Sanctuary** (tel: (727) 391 6211) where injured birds are nursed back to health.

### TAMPA BAY HISTORY CENTER

The glass-and-steel high rises of downtown Tampa do little to evoke the area's history but 12,000 years of local settlement are featured at the Tampa Bay History Center, at the corner of Franklin and Platt streets. The exhibited maps, military uniforms, photos and artefacts reveal the area's rise from swampy outpost to thriving modern city. The center is open 10:00–17:00 Tuesday–Saturday, 13:00–17:00 Sunday; admission free.

**Above:** *The spotting of manatees is possible off Anna Maria Island's pier.*
**Opposite:** *The impressive, well-kept grounds of the John and Mable Ringling Museum in Sarasota.*

## MANATEE SPOTTING

Unfortunately the sea cow population is declining, but these gentle creatures still frequent the Gulf Coast. Good places to spot them include: **Terra Ceia Bay** at Sea Breeze Point; **Snead Island Emerson Point; Palma Sola Bay** on the Causeway and at Rose Park; **Manatee River;** Kingfish boat ramp, Coquina Beach Park, Leffis Key and Bayfront Park, all on **Anna Maria Island**. Sightings are guaranteed at the **South Florida Museum** in Bradenton.

### BRADENTON

The area was first inhabited by Timucuan Indians and, although visited by Spanish explorers, was not developed until 1842. Josiah Gates was the county's first permanent settler and **Major Robert Gamble** soon joined him. Gamble's house and huge plantation (the only surviving Antebellum plantation) can be visited on Patten Avenue in Bradenton. Open 09:00–17:00 Thursday–Monday. Guided tours 09:30, 10:30, 13:00–16:00 Thursday–Monday.

Set inland from the Gulf of Mexico, at the mouth of the Manatee River, Bradenton proudly preserves its historical roots. **Manatee Village Historical Park**, on Manatee Avenue takes visitors back in time with its carefully restored buildings. A memorial on 75th Street is dedicated to Hernando de Soto, the first Spaniard to land here, and the **South Florida Museum, Bishop Planetarium and Parker Manatee Aquarium** on 10th Street West covers the history of Florida from the Stone Age to the Space Age.

From Bradenton you can also enjoy a 75-minute ride aboard the **Florida Gulf Coast Railroad**. Alternatively, the world's largest airboat is available for trips through the **Myakka River State Park**, a dense woodland along the Myakka River and a breeding ground for numerous birds, which lies between Bradenton and Sarasota on Highway 72. The park is open from 08:00 until sunset; tel: (941) 361-6511.

# SARASOTA

Sarasota considers itself the cultural capital of Florida, thanks in no small way to the influence of grand circus master **John Ringling** and his wife Mable. The city is home to the Florida West Coast Symphony and offers a marvellous host of artistic venues, such as the beautiful **Asolo Performing Arts Center** and the **Van Wezel Performing Arts Hall**.

The **Asolo Theater** is a 19th-century playhouse that was partly shipped from Asolo in Italy and was reconstructed in the United States. It is situated just up the road from **Bellm's Cars and Music of Yesterday**, which features an interesting collection of antique cars and more than 1500 musical antiques. Open 09:30–17:30 daily. The city's symphony orchestra performs regularly and there is a varied programme of fine opera and ballet productions. An annual jazz festival is held each April, as well as other community events such as the annual premier of the new circus season, dedicated to the memory of the famous Ringlings. Their Venetian-style winter home, **Ca'd'Zan**, which they designed after a visit to Europe, is open to the public and gives a taste of the wealth and glitz of the 1920s. Open 10:00–17:30 daily.

The adjacent **John and Mable Ringling Museum of Art** employs volunteer guides to take visitors around the 22-gallery maze of Old Masters and contemporary artworks, the classical courtyards adorned with statues, and Mable Ringling's fine rose garden. In honour of their circus background, the Ringlings also gave Sarasota the lovely **Circus Galleries** museum, housing gaily painted parade wagons, costumes and other circus memorabilia. Open 10:00–17:30 daily.

## BARRIER ISLANDS

**Egmont Key:** uninhabited island in Tampa Bay, with white, sandy beaches, a large population of turtles and excellent beachcombing.
**Anna Maria Island:** a 7-mile (11km) island with a distinctly laid-back Caribbean feel.
**Longboat Key:** tennis and golf are the main attractions on this island, which also holds the Mote Marine Aquarium and Pelican Man's Bird Sanctuary.
**Lido and St Armands Keys:** resort area with glitzy shops and restaurants.
**Siesta Key:** powdery sand and Point Rock, which is known for sponges, colourful shells and tropical fish.

## MARCO ISLAND

Marco Island, 16 miles (26km) south of Naples, is the largest and only developed island of the Ten Thousand Island chain that runs down to the Florida Keys. Take a **trolley tour** to explore the island, dine out in one of the many excellent seafood restaurants or shop in the quaint old-style shopping centres. Indian burial mounds and a history of providing sanctuary for pirates gives the island plenty of folklore – and promise of buried treasure.

**Below:** *The Castaways Beach Plantation on Sanibel Island.*

## FORT MYERS

Fort Myers, developed during the Indian wars, started to grow in the late 1880s when tourists began to flock in.

### The Edison and Ford Winter Estates ★★

Among the first arrivals was **Thomas Edison** who built a retreat on McGregor Boulevard in 1885. Adjacent to the house is a fascinating museum displaying hundreds of his inventions (some of the original light bulbs still burn). Tours only: 09:00–16:00 daily. Next door is Henry Ford's winter home, **Mangoes**. You can buy combination tickets to see both homes.

A few miles away is the **Southwest Florida Museum of History** with an interesting collection of Calusa Indian artefacts and Ethel Cooper glass. Parked outside is the *Esperanza*, longest and last of the Pullman coaches.

North of town lies the **Babcock Wilderness Adventures**, where you can join a 90-minute swamp-buggy tour and see bison, alligators, panthers, wild turkey and deer.

### Sanibel Island ★

Explore the **JN 'Ding' Darling National Wildlife Refuge**, where there is a four-mile (6km) drive alongside mangrove swamps as well as walkways, and cycling and canoe trails. Sanibel Island has five public beaches and the **Bailey-Matthews Shell Museum** (3075 Sanibel-Captiva Road), which holds about two million land and sea shells. Open 10:00–16:00 daily. Enthusiasts eager to collect their own may pick only dead shells on the beaches of Sanibel and Captiva. The best area is reputed to be the 'shell line', where the highest waves break on the beach. Please take note that a law introduced in 1995 strictly prohibits the gathering of live specimens.

## AROUND NAPLES

The city of Naples is really the main resort area of this wonderful stretch of the coast. It lies between the Gulf of Mexico and the Everglades, right at the northern tip of the **Ten Thousand Island** chain that runs down to the Florida Keys. Only **Marco Island** is developed.

## Naples ★

Naples itself has little to offer in the way of museums or attractions, though the surrounding country has a wealth of places to explore. One exceptions in the

city is the **Collier County Museum** which displays the history of the region from prehistoric to modern times.

The **Teddy Bear Museum** of Naples, on 2511 Pine Ridge Road, features a collection of more than 3000 lovable cuddly furry toys from around the world, displayed in a variety of novel poses.

The **Philharmonic Center for the Arts**, situated on Pelican Bay Boulevard, is the regional hub for the arts and music with four art galleries and two sculpture gardens, as well as a full yearly programme of events.

## Sanctuaries ★★

To explore the peaceful surrounding countryside, visit the **Conservancy of Southwest Florida's Naples Nature Center** on 1450 Merrihue Drive, where there are aquariums and a serpentarium. Boat tours are available from here. Or you can head 20 miles (32km) north of Naples to the **Corkscrew Swamp Sanctuary** where alligators, bobcats and otters live among giant bald cypress trees several hundreds of years old. The teeming birdlife will delight novices and ornithologists alike, and is best observed in winter when the birds tend to flock around the remaining pools of water.

**Above:** *Idyllic sands and sea in the Fort Myers area.*

### BARRIER ISLANDS

**Boca Grande:** a retreat for the rich who enjoy its 19th-century atmosphere of wooden houses and sleepy fishing village.

**Cabbage Key:** a Calusa Indian shell mound lies under an inn built by playwright Mary Roberts Rinehart.

**Sanibel:** two-thirds of the island is dedicated to the **JN 'Ding' Darling National Wildlife Refuge**, named after a Pulitzer prize-winning cartoonist; shell-collecting here is exceptional.

**Gasparilla:** was once a favourite pirate haven.

**Captiva:** very popular among shell-seekers.

**Useppa:** a historic island retreat featuring the restored 100-year-old Collier Inn.

# The West Coast at a Glance

Locals pride themselves on the annual **360 days** of **sunshine**. Temperatures rarely fall below 60°F (15°C). In mid-summer 90°F (32°C) is common, but tempered by cool sea breezes. Near the **Everglades** it is rainy and humid in summer, with swarms of mosquitoes.

**Tampa International Airport** is rapidly expanding to cope with demand from Europe. It also has good US connections. The **Sarasota–Bradenton International Airport** is well served by American carriers. **Southwest Florida International Airport** has also expanded and serves the Fort Myers area. **Car rental** companies are found at convenient locations. Hotels operate airport **shuttle buses**. By car you reach the West Coast off **Interstate 75** (north–south) and from **Interstate 4** (heading west from Daytona Beach and Orlando.) **Highway 19** hugs the coast from Tallahassee to St Petersburg. **Highway 41** goes to Naples. From Miami the **Tamiami Trail** runs west to Naples. The **Everglades Parkway** connects Fort Lauderdale with Naples. **Greyhound:** good interstate service stops in Tampa, Sarasota, St Petersburg and Fort Myers.

**Road** networks are good and it is easy to cross the state to Orlando and the theme parks or down to the Everglades.

The cities all have local **bus** networks. Clearwater Beach and Fort Myers Beach have **trolley services,** and **ferries** operate between the islands.

*Tampa*
LUXURY
**Wyndham Harbour Island**, 725 S Harbour Island Blvd, tel: (813) 229-5000, fax: 229-5322. Rooms overlook the bay; walking distance to downtown.
MID-RANGE
**Holiday Inn Tampa Busch Gardens**, 2701 E Fowler Ave, tel: (813) 971-4710, fax: 979-0951. Close to theme park.

*St Petersburg*
LUXURY
**Don CeSar Beach Resort**, 3400 Gulf Blvd, St Pete Beach, tel: (727) 360-1881, fax: 367-6952. Used by F Scott Fitzgerald and Al Capone.
MID-RANGE
**Howard Johnson Resort Hotel**, 6100 Gulf Blvd, tel: (727) 360-7041. 116-room hotel with beach access.
BUDGET
**Lamara Hotel Apartments**, 520 73rd Ave, tel: (727) 360-7521. Small hotel/motel with beach access and low rates.

*Clearwater Area*
LUXURY
**The Clearwater Beach Hotel**, 500 Mandalay Ave, tel: (727) 441-2425, www.clearwater-beachhotel.com Overlooks Gulf of Mexico; private beach.

MID-RANGE
**Best Western Sea Wake Inn**, 691 S Gulfview Blvd, Clearwater Beach, tel: (727) 443-7652, web: www.best western.com On the beach.
BUDGET
**Chart House Suites**, 850 Bay Way Blvd, Clearwater Beach, tel: (727) 449-8007, fax: 443-6081. Overlooks the bay.

*Sarasota Area*
LUXURY
**Hyatt Sarasota**, 1000 Blvd of the Arts, tel: (941) 953-1234, web: www.sarasota.hyatt.com In city centre; some rooms overlook bay area.
MID-RANGE
**The Helmsley Sandcastle Hotel**, 1540 Ben Franklin Dr, tel: (941) 388-2181, web: www.helmsleysandcastle.com Beside beach on Lido Key.

*Fort Myers*
LUXURY
**Sanibel Harbour Resort & Spa**, 17260 Harbour Pointe Dr, tel: (239) 466-4000, web: www.sanibel-resort.com Overlooks Sanibel and Captiva islands.
MID-RANGE
**Howard Johnson**, 4811 S. Cleveland Ave, tel: (239) 936-3229, web: www.howard johnsonfortmyers.com Affordable and accessible.
BUDGET
**Comfort Inn**, 4171 Boatways Rd, tel: (239) 694-9200, web: www.choicehotels.com An ideal choice for business and relaxation.

# The West Coast at a Glance

## Naples

### LUXURY

**La Playa Beach Resort**, 9891 Gulf Shore Dr, tel: (239) 597-3123, www.laplayaresort.com This resort targets golfers and honeymooners; ther are rooms with sunset view.

**The Registry Resort**, 475 Seagate Dr, tel: (239) 597-3232, www.registryresort.com Luxury resort; has shuttle through mangroves to beach.

### MID-RANGE

**Vanderbilt Beach Resort**, 9225 Gulfshore Dr, tel: (239) 597-3144, www.vanderbiltbeach resort.com Beachfront motel with dock and boat ramp.

### BUDGET

**Inn at Pelican Bay**, 800 Vanderbilt Beach Rd, tel: (239) 597-8777, www.innatpelicanbay.com Small hotel with European style.

### WHERE TO EAT

## Tampa

**Columbia Restaurant**, 2117 E 7th Ave, Ybor City, tel: (813) 248-4961. This claims to be America's oldest Spanish restaurant.

**Ceviche Restaurant & Tapas Bar**, 2109 Bayshore Blvd, tel: (813) 250-0203. Serving Spanish cuisine nightly.

## St Petersburg

**Hurricane**, 9th Ave and Gulf Way, tel: (727) 360-9558. Very casual, excellent seafood.

**Wine Cellar**, 17307 Gulf Blvd, N Redington Beach, tel: (727) 393-3491. International menu, highly acclaimed.

## Clearwater

**Bascom's Chop House**, 3665 Ulmerton Rd, Clearwater, tel: (727) 573-3363, web: www.bascoms.com American cuisine; smart, with dress code. Reservations recommended.

**Hogfish Grill**, 1800 Gulf to Bay Blvd, tel: (727) 446-7027. Winning accolades for its barbeque seafood.

## Sarasota Area

**Columbia Restaurant**, 411 St Armands Circle, tel: (941) 388-3987, web: www.columbia restaurant.com Reservations required; long-standing reputation for Spanish/Cuban cuisine.

**Marina Jack**, 2 Marina Plaza, tel: (941) 365-4232, web: www.marinajacks.com Outdoor waterfront dining in downtown area, children welcome. Good value during the day, more expensive in the evening.

## Captiva Island

**The Bubble Room**, 15001 Captiva Dr, tel: (239) 472-5558, web: www.bubbleroom restaurant.com

## Naples

**Dock Restaurant**, 845 12th Ave S., tel: (239) 263-9940, Waterfront dining, happy hour, children welcome, gift shop.

**Ridgway Bar & Grill**, 1300 Third St, tel: (239) 262-5500, web: www.ridgwaybarandgrill.com Open all day; classic American; children welcome; reservations recommended.

### SHOPPING

**Centro Ybor**, 1600 E 8th St, Tampa, tel: (813) 242-4660. In the centre of the historic area.

**International Plaza & Bay St**, 2223 N Westshore Blvd, Tampa, tel: (813) 342-3790.

**Prime Outlets at Naples**, 6060 Collier Blvd, Naples, tel: (239) 775-8083, discounted prices.

### TOURS AND EXCURSIONS

**Around The Bend Nature Tours**, 1815 Palma Sola Blvd, Bradenton, tel: (941) 794-8773, www.aroundbend.com

**Skydive City**, 4241 SkyDive Ln, Zephyrhills, tel: (813) 783-9399, www.skydivecity.com

**Baseball** spring training camps; Tampa Bay Buccanneers offer NFL games.

### USEFUL CONTACTS

**Convention and Visitors Bureau Information Centers:**

**Beaches of Fort Myers & Sanibel**, 12800 University Dr, Suite 550, Fort Myers, 33907, tel: (239) 338-3500, web: www.FortMyersSanibel.com UK, tel: 01273 832832.

**Tampa Bay**, 615 Channelside Dr, tel: (813) 223-2752, www.VisitTampaBay.com

**St Petersburg/Clearwater Area**, 14450–46th St, Suite 108, Clearwater, tel: (727) 464-7200, www.floridas-beach.com

**Bradenton Area**, One Haben Blvd, Palmetto tel: (941) 729-9177, www.flagulfislands.com

**Sarasota**, 655 N Tamiami Trail, tel: 0800 522 9799, www.sarasotafl.org

# 8
# The Florida Keys

The Florida Keys and Key West, to give the area its correct name, is an approximately 180-mile (290km) chain of islands trailing off Florida's southeastern tip and arcing to the southwest into the Atlantic. The northern-most island of **Key Largo** is the land base for the **John Pennekamp Coral Reef State Park**. The most southerly point, the **Dry Tortugas**, lies just about 85 miles (137km) north of Havana, Cuba.

An official count for the number of islands is unavailable, but estimates put the total at around 800, spread over 2700 sq miles (6995km²) of coral reefs. Forty-two of the islands are linked by the 113 mile (182km) US1, or **Overseas Highway**, which spans 43 bridges including the famous **Seven Mile Bridge**.

Despite the road link, most of the islands are accessible only by water. This has ensured that the region is able to preserve a feeling of the past; today all the islands are protected by the **Florida Keys National Marine Sanctuary**. Fishing, sunning and snorkelling are still the main activities and nightlife is limited to eating out and sampling the different bars. The atmosphere is unlike that in any other part of Florida – this could easily be the Caribbean, rather than the United States.

One of this region's most famous residents, author **Ernest Hemingway**, has come to epitomize the lifestyle of the Keys, and little has changed since he lived, wrote and fished here – except for the growing number of visitors who head south to try and capture the spirit of these beguiling, laid-back islands.

## DON'T MISS

*** The Dolphin Research Center, Grassy Key:** inspired the popular movie *Flipper*.
**** The Wrecker's Museum, Key West:** pirate mementos, and marine artefacts.
**** Mallory Square, Key West:** admire the sunset.
**** John Pennekamp State Park, Key Largo:** first under-water state park; America's only living coral reef.
*** African Queen, Key Largo:** original boat used by Humphrey Bogart and Katharine Hepburn in the movie *African Queen*.

**Opposite:** *Underwater adventures abound in the Florida Keys.*

## KEY LARGO

The largest island in the chain at nearly 30 miles (48km) long, Key Largo is also the most developed. Key Largo claims to be the **diving capital** of the United States and, while this title might be disputed by some, there's no doubt the place is popular with divers.

The **John Pennekamp Coral Reef State Park** was the very first underwater sanctuary in America, established in order to protect part of the only living coral reef in the United States. It covers 53,661 acres (21,716ha) of submerged land as well as 2350 acres (951ha) above water. Visitors can enjoy a full range of water sports and sightseeing activities. The wonderland of 500 species of fish and 55 varieties of coral is also accessible to non-swimmers via glass-bottom boats.

Land-based attractions include the **Crocodile Lakes National Wildlife Refuge**.

In historical Tavernier, the station, churches and pioneer homes date back to the turn of the century.

### CLIMATE

Winter (December–April) lows average 65°–70°F (18°–21°C). **Summer** (July–October) is **hot** and **humid** with highs around 90°F (32°C). **Hurricane season** is from **August–October**.

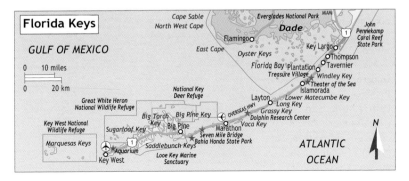

## THE UPPER KEYS
### Windley Key ★★

After passing through **Plantation Key**, named for its many tropical fruit farms, you reach **Windley Key** and the **Theater of the Sea**. Here you can see dolphins, even swim alongside them (by prior appointment, for the over-13s, and only after a 30-minute orientation crash course), or meet a live shark. There is a 'bottomless' boat to ride, as well as entertaining dolphin and sea lion shows. A new attraction is the **Trainer for a Day** programme which includes three hours of caring for and feeding the dolphins, with lessons on anatomy, physiology and dolphin behaviour. Open 09:30–16:00 daily.

The **Hurricane Memorial** at MM82 (Mile Marker 82) marks the mass grave of 423 construction workers who lost their lives during the 1935 Labor Day hurricane. **Windley Key Fossil Reef Geological Site** at MM85.3 offers free tours of a 30-acre (12ha) area of pristine hummocks, fauna and archaeological sites.

### Islamorada ★

Billed as the **sport fishing capital** of the world, this is the perfect base for deep-sea fishing expeditions. Marlin, tuna and dolphin (a fish – also called *mahi-mahi* – and not the mammal) are found just offshore in the Atlantic, while tarpon and bonefish offer shallow-water challenges.

South of Islamorada lies Long Key and the lovely **Long Key State Recreation Area**, a place to relax, fish, swim, go canoeing or walking. Book ahead for the camping facilities, particularly in peak season.

Nearby, at the **San Pedro Underwater Archaeological Preserve**, lies the 287-ton Dutch-built *San Pedro* which sank in 1733. Rediscovered in 1960 in 18ft (5½m) of water, much of the wreck was hauled back

**Opposite:** *The Christ of the Abyss, 25ft (8m) underwater at John Pennekamp Coral Reef State Park.*

**Below:** *Idyllic island life on Upper Matecumbe Key.*

to the surface. Today it is a very popular dive site with a pile of ballast stones to mark the spot, as well as replica cannons, an anchor and an underwater information plate.

## Marathon ★

Before reaching Marathon, at MM59 on Grassy Key is the **Dolphin Research Center**, which works with universities and research facilities around the world. Here too, you can swim with the dolphins but need to book well ahead (at least a month before your intended visit). This was once the site of Flipper's Sea School for training dolphins and here the original 1950s *Flipper* movie was filmed.

Marathon itself has an excellent natural history museum, and the **Crane Point Hammock**, an archaeological site with finds dating back some seven centuries, and the oldest example of Conch-style architecture outside of Key West. Short walking trails from the museum weave through the tropical forest that holds the historic sites.

Driving south from Marathon, you cross the famous **Seven Mile Bridge** which actually measures only 6.9 miles (11km). It was completed in 1982 at a cost of US$45 million and is the world's longest segmental bridge. Every April, runners gather in Marathon for a special bridge race. At MM47 lies the pedestrian entrance to the **Old Seven Mile Bridge**. The structure is listed on the National Register of Historic Places and, across the Middle to Lower Keys, it rests on 546 concrete pillars.

## THE LOWER KEYS

The area from Seven Mile Bridge south to Key West is known as the **Lower Keys**. This is what people dream of when they think of the Keys: peace and quiet, stunning views and undisturbed wildlife. Parks include the **Bahia Honda State Park** with cabins and camp sites overlooking the ocean, the **Looe Key National Marine Sanctuary** named after the HMS *Looe* which ran aground here in 1744, and the **National Key Deer Refuge**, which is home to several hundred miniature deer. A subspecies of the Virginia white-tailed deer, this little animal has been under threat from encroaching human development and traffic on the main highway.

**Above:** *The strange Ripley's Believe It or Not!® in Duval Street, Key West.*
**Opposite:** *Catch of the day – a huge marlin caught off the Florida Keys.*

### Key West ★★★

Key West has become a legend in its own lifetime, a place people visit to experience something different. Once a barely accessible paradise for escapists, Key West has since been forced into the mainstream by hordes of tourists yet retains some of the quirkiness that makes it so unique.

In April 1982 the United States Border Patrol set up roadblocks across the Overseas Highway just south of Florida City in an attempt to stem the flow of illegal aliens from here into the United States. Traffic chaos ensued as police searched every vehicle, demanding occupants produce proof of their US citizenship. In protest at being treated like foreigners in their own country, city officials of Key West proclaimed the **Conch Republic**, complete with separate flag, mock visas, border passes and currency, forcing a chagrined border patrol to beat a hasty retreat. 'Conch' passports and visas are still available from the Key West Chamber of Commerce and the Conch Republic Celebration, in honour of the 'secessionists victory', is held in April every year.

Always out on a limb, the Key West inhabitants started out as **wreckers**, aiding the victims of shipwrecks and rescuing cargo, though stories of deliberate wrecking abound.

---

**FORMER CAPITAL**

**Indian Key**, on the Atlantic side of Islamorada, was once the home of native American tribes. In 1831 Jacob Housman bought the island as a base for his wrecking business and eventually added a hotel, wharves and warehouses. The population thrived, and for a short time the island was the **capital of Dade**, the county that includes Miami. But it all came to a bloody end on 7 August 1840 when native Americans, angered by the loss of territory that had been theirs for centuries, attacked the town and butchered most of its residents. Since then the island has remained uninhabited; accessible by boat only.

Its uniqueness has subsequently appealed to eccentrics and celebrities. The committed environmentalist **John Audubon** started preservation awareness and helped retain much of the history of the island. **Ernest Hemingway** found inspiration for much of his work while living here.

Key West is hedonism at its best. In the evening, head down **Duval Street** to festive **Mallory Square**, where locals and tourists mingle with jugglers, fire eaters and buskers, as the sun sets to a round of applause. Mallory Square forms the starting point for lively evenings out in the many bars, cafés and restaurants, most of which have live music with a Caribbean flavour.

During the day, a good place to start a tour is on Truman Avenue. Turn left on Lean Street to find the home of playwright **Tennessee Williams**. Continue down Truman Avenue and turn left into **Whitehead Street** to reach the most southerly point of mainland America accessible to the public. Turn right to find the **Lighthouse Museum** where you can climb 98 steps for lovely views across the island and out to sea.

### END OF THE ROAD

The cluster of islands lying beyond Key West is called the **Dry Tortugas**. Known as the Gibraltar of the Gulf due to their strategic position, they were of prime military importance in the past. Fort Jefferson on Garden Key has artillery tiers for 450 guns and 50ft (15m) walls 8ft (2½m) thick. Used as a prison after the Civil War, it is now a tourist site.

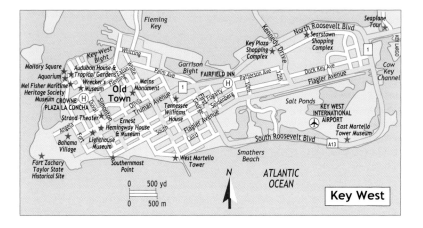

Almost opposite is the unusual **Hemingway House** (open 09:00–17:00 daily). Dating back to 1851, this was the famous author's home from 1931 to 1940. It was the first house in Key West to have running water, a fireplace and a pool. The headboard of the bed is made from a 17th-century Spanish monastery gate, the glass chandelier was hand-blown and the Picasso cat was a gift to the author from Pablo Picasso himself. The house is now a museum and inhabited by 42 cats (most with six toes or more), one for each bridge in the Keys.

Left off Whitehead and into Petronia Street, you reach the lively Caribbean-style **Bahama Village** neighbourhood. Further north, at the corner of Whitehead Street and **Greene Street**, among a row of irresistibly quaint 'gingerbread' conch-style houses, is the **Audubon House**, filled with a priceless collection of furniture from the mid-1800s and original bird engravings by the artist. Open 09:30–17:00 daily.

Opposite is the **Mel Fisher Maritime Heritage Society Museum**, housing treasure that was lost by two Spanish galleons which foundered during a hurricane in 1622. Just down the road, back on Duval Street, is the **Wrecker's Museum**, built in 1829 for Florida Senator Watlington, who was also a sea captain and wrecker. The house is said to be the oldest in Key West.

The delightful pink and green house at the end of the street is often called the Southernmost House. This is actually a misnomer, since another one was erected just south of it. And maintaining its eco-credentials, the latest in Key West is the Florida Keys Eco-Discovery Center on the waterfront at Truman Annex. Highlights include a walk-through version of the Aquaris Undersea Lab while the whole attraction has plenty of interactive exhibits to showcase the underwater world around the Keys.

> **HEMINGWAY DAYS**
>
> Ernest 'Papa' Hemingway wrote *For Whom the Bell Tolls*, *The Green Hills of Africa*, *The Snows of Kilimanjaro*, *Death in the Afternoon* and *The Old Man and the Sea* while living on Whitehead Street in Key West, between organizing boxing matches and drinking at Sloppy Joe's.

**Opposite:** *Famous author, Ernest Hemingway, accessed his study via a catwalk.*
**Below:** *Aerial view of Fort Jefferson (Dry Tortugas).*

# The Florida Keys at a Glance

## BEST TIMES TO VISIT

The climate is kinder in the Keys than on the mainland. **Summer** temperatures reach 80°F (27°C) in July and drop to around 70°F (21°C) in the winter. Winds keep the islands **free of humidity** in summer and warm in winter. **Hurricane** season extends from **August** to **October** and tropical storms occur throughout the summer months. The Keys are busy in winter, but limited accommodation keeps tourist numbers to manageable levels.

## GETTING THERE

**Key West International Airport** is on the southeast corner of the island, while **Marathon Airport** is on Marathon at MM52. Direct international flights into the Keys are not available and most visitors use Miami as a gateway – flying time is 45 minutes to Key West and 35 minutes to Marathon. The majority of visitors arrive by car. The only road to the Keys is **Highway 1** (the Overseas Highway), which heads south out of Florida City and continues down to Key West across 43 bridges. This road is marked per mile, directions are given by **Mile Marker** (MM) with MM1 on the tip of Key West. There is no train service, since the line was destroyed by a hurricane in the 1930s, but you can arrive by yacht or cruise line.

## GETTING AROUND

Most of the islands are small enough to explore on foot, but taxis are available. Key West has two tourist services, known as: **Conch Tour Train**, tel: (305) 294-5161 and **Old Town Trolley**, 1910 N Roosevelt Blvd, tel: (305) 296-6688. Both of these take about 90 minutes to tour the town.

## WHERE TO STAY

You should book ahead for any establishment in the Keys. The relatively few hotels are extremely popular, particularly around Christmas, in the summer season and on United States holiday weekends.

### Key Largo
*LUXURY*
**Holiday Inn Key Largo Resort and Marina**, 99701 Overseas Highway, tel: (305) 451-2121, fax: 451-5592. Renovated by the man who also restored the *African Queen*, moored outside.
**Marriott Key Largo Bay Beach Resort**, 103800 Overseas Highway, tel (305) 453-0000. Luxurious resort on the beach.

*MID-RANGE*
**Marina del Mar Resort and Marina**, 527 Caribbean Dr, Key Largo, tel: (305) 451-4107, fax: 451-1891.Offers a deepwater marina; with some of the world's best diving nearby.

**Ocean Point Suites**, 500 Burton Dr, Key Largo, tel: (305) 853-3000.

### Islamorada
*LUXURY*
**Cheeca Lodge**, MM82, Upper Matecumbe Key, tel: (305) 664-4651, fax: 664-2893. Won awards for its environmentally friendly schemes. Calm and spacious.

*MID-RANGE*
**Casa Morada**, 136 Madeira Road, tel: (305) 664-0044.
**Pelican Cove**, 84457 Old Overseas Highway, tel: (305) 664-4435.

### Duck Key
*LUXURY*
**Hawk's Cay Resort**, tel: (305) 743-7000. With dolphin experience.
**Faro Blanco Marine Resort**, tel: (305) 743-9018.

*MID-RANGE*
**Banana Bay Resort and Marina**, 4590 Overseas Highway, tel: (305) 743-3500, fax: 743-2670. A beautiful and very relaxing resort.
**Sombero Resort and Lighthouse Marina**, 19 Sombero Beach Blvd, tel: (305) 743-2250, fax: 743-2998. Suites all have kitchens, good marina.

*BUDGET*
**Seascape Oceanfront Resort**, tel: (305) 743-6455.
**Howard Johnson Resort**, tel: toll-free (800) 321-3496.

## The Florida Keys at a Glance

### Key West

**LUXURY**

**The Banyan Resort**, 323 Whitehead St, tel: (305) 296-7786, fax: 294-1107. Within walking distance of Old Town attractions; pleasant gardens.

**Crowne Plaza La Concha**, 430 Duval St, tel: (305) 296-2991, fax: 294-3283. Seven storeys of Art Deco; guests have included Ernest Hemingway and Tennessee Williams.

**Fairfield Inn**, 2400 N Roosevelt Blvd, tel: (305) 296-5700, fax: 292-9840. Free breakfast, two pools and only a mile from downtown.

### WHERE TO EAT

The Keys have their very own cuisine with an emphasis on seafood. Eat stone crabs in season (15 Oct–15 May), when they can legally be harvested. Definitely sample Key lime pie.

### Key Largo

**Mrs Mac's Kitchen**, MM99, tel: (305) 451-3722. Good food; lovely international decor.

### Islamorada

**Marker 88 Restaurant**, tel: (305) 852-9315. Casual but costly, award-winning food in a tropical setting.

### Marathon

**Grassy Key Dairy Bar**, MM58.5, tel: (305) 743-3816. Good food at good prices.

**Kelsey's**, M48, 1996 Overseas Highway, Docks of Faro Blanco Resort, tel: (305)

743-9018. Beautiful setting, overlooking ocean; local dishes a speciality.

### Key West

**Pepe's Cafe and Steak House**, 806 Caroline St, tel: (305) 294-7192. Best place in town for breakfast; meet locals in this small shack which serves affordable meals all day long.

**Half Shell Raw Bar**, Land's End Marina, tel: (305) 294-7496. Huge plates of oysters and conch chowder are two of the best dishes.

**Sloppy Joe's**, 201 Duval St, tel: (305) 294-8585. Former haunt of Ernest Hemingway, now a tourist trap but still a 'must see'.

### SHOPPING

Not much exciting shopping is to be had in the Keys, beyond the normal resort shops, and souvenir T-shirt stalls.

**Mallory Square**, Key West, tel: (305) 296-4557. Main centre, .

**The Rain Barrel**, Islamorada. Art show in March with 100 artists and some 20,000 visitors.

**Fast Buck Freddie's**, 500 Duval St. A Greenpeace outpost selling rather offbeat items like Pelican Poop.

### TOURS AND EXCURSIONS

**Yankee Freedom II Dry Tortugas National Park Ferry**, 240 Margaret St, Key West, tel: (305) 294-7009. Cruise on a 100ft catamaran to Fort Jefferson and the Dry Tortugas.

**Old Town Trolley Tours**, Mallory Square, Key West, tel: (305) 296-6688. 90-minute tour of attractions with 12 stops along the way.

**Conch Tour Train**, 501 Front St, Key West, tel: (305) 294-5161. 90-minute tours.

### USEFUL CONTACTS

**Florida Keys and Key West Development Council**, 1201 White St, tel: (305) 296-1552, web: www.fla-keys.co.uk

**Key West Information Center**, 1601 N Roosevelt Blvd, Key West, tel: (305) 292-5000, web: www.keywestinfo.com

**Key Largo Chamber of Commerce/Florida Keys Visitor Center**, 106000 Overseas Hwy, Key Largo, tel: (305) 451-1414, web: www.keylargochamber.org

**Coast Guard Group Key West**, tel: (305) 292-8727. Information on navigational hazards, safety and weather.

| KEY WEST | J | F | M | A | M | J | J | A | S | O | N | D |
|---|---|---|---|---|---|---|---|---|---|---|---|---|
| AVERAGE TEMP. °F | 65 | 67 | 68 | 72 | 74 | 77 | 79 | 79 | 77 | 76 | 70 | 67 |
| AVERAGE TEMP. °C | 18 | 19 | 20 | 22 | 23 | 25 | 26 | 26 | 25 | 24 | 21 | 19 |
| HOURS OF SUN DAILY | 12 | 12 | 12 | 13 | 13 | 14 | 14 | 14 | 13 | 12 | 12 | 12 |
| RAINFALL in | 2 | 2 | 2 | 3 | 6.5 | 9 | 6 | 7 | 8 | 7 | 2.5 | 2 |
| RAINFALL mm | 51 | 51 | 51 | 76 | 165 | 229 | 152 | 179 | 203 | 179 | 63 | 51 |
| DAYS OF RAINFALL | 7 | 7 | 7 | 8 | 12 | 15 | 13 | 13 | 14 | 13 | 8 | 7 |

# Travel Tips

## Tourist Information

The Florida Commission on Tourism (represented as Visit Florida) has branches in London, Paris, Toronto and in South America. The **London** office receives personal callers by prior appointment only, tel: 020 7932 2406. For a free Florida information pack tel: 01737 644882. The head office is in **Tallahassee**, Suite 30D, 661 East Jefferson St, tel: (850) 488-5607, www.FLAUSA.com Each county and city has its own separate tourism office.
Beaches of **Fort Myers & Sanibel** – Lee County Visitor and Convention Bureau, tel: (239) 338-3500, www.FortMyersSanibel.com
Greater **Miami** Convention and Visitors Bureau, tel: (305) 539-3000, www. miamiandbeaches.com
Greater **Fort Lauderdale** Convention and Visitors Bureau, tel: (954) 765-4466, www.sunny.org
**Tampa Bay** Convention and Visitors Bureau, tel: (813) 223-2752, www.VisitTampaBay.com
**Tallahassee Area** Convention and Visitors Bureau, tel: (850) 606-2305, www.visittallahassee.com

**St Petersburg–Clearwater** Area Convention and Visitors Bureau, tel: (727) 464-7200, www.floridasbeach.com
**Orlando–Orange County** Convention and Visitors Bureau, tel: (407) 363-5872, from UK call freephone: 0800 018 6760, www.orlando info.com
**Kissimmee** Convention and Visitors **Bureau**, tel: (407) 847-5000, www.floridakiss.com
**Daytona Beach Area** Convention and Visitors Bureau, tel: (386) 255-0415, www.daytonabeach.com
**Jacksonville and the Beaches** Convention and Visitors Bureau, tel: (904) 798-9111, www.visitjacksonville.com
**Florida Keys and Key West** Development Council, 1201 White St, tel: (305) 296-1552, www.fla-keys.co.uk
Information about attractions can be obtained from **Florida Attractions Association**, Box 10295, Tallahassee FL32302, tel: (850) 222-2885. Information about state parks and recreation areas comes from **Office of Recreation and Parks**, Mail Station 535, 3900 Commonwealth Blvd, Tallahassee, FL32399-3000, tel: (850) 488-9872.

## Entry Requirements

Since 9/11, security systems have been tightened. Visitors should **check the latest rules before travelling** but, at the time of print, visitors must be in possession of a valid machine readable passport and be able to show a return air ticket. EU citizens may enter the US under the visa waiver scheme and will be given the necessary forms as they enter the country. Anyone on a fly-drive vacation must have an address for the first night. All children now need to travel on their own passport. Anyone staying longer than 90 days must have a visa. Citizens other than those from Britain, New Zealand, Japan and most western European countries need a valid passport that expires at least six months after their visit to the US has ended. Multiple re-entry visas are valid for 10 years and can be transferred to new passports. Visa costs vary according to nationality. Those with multiple re-entry visas will be able to enter blue lanes at immigration points, which should be quicker.
In Britain, visas can be obtained in writing from the **Visa and Immigration Dept of the**

**United States**, United States Embassy, 5 Upper Grosvenor St, London W1A 2JB, tel: (020 7) 499-3443.

## Customs

Customs forms have to be completed before arrival. Familiar red and green channels greet visitors at the airport. Allowances for non-resident adults (over 21) are: 1 litre spirits, 200 cigarettes or 50 cigars or 2kg of tobacco, and 100ml of perfume. Unlicensed importation of fruit, plants and meat is banned – travel snacks like apples will be confiscated.

## Health Requirements

No vaccinations are required to enter the US, unless coming from an area suffering from outbreaks of cholera or yellow fever. However, adequate health insurance cover is essential. Florida has a very good health and dental care system but it is extremely expensive. Carry a doctor's prescription to allay fears of drug smuggling if you are on medication involving narcotics or syringes.

## Getting There

**By Air:** All main US carriers fly into Florida. The major gateways from Europe are Miami International Airport and Orlando International Airport, although an increasing amount of traffic is handled by Tampa. St Petersburg and Sanford international airports receive charter flights from Europe. All the bigger cities have regional airports with extensive connections from the main entry points into

Florida and from other parts of the United States.

**By Road:** The network of the efficient Greyhound bus service extends all over the United States and into Florida.

**By Rail:** Amtrak operates a national service, though few areas in Florida are connected. The main railway line runs down to Miami but bypasses some of the central east coast. There are no links through the Everglades or into the Keys.

**By Boat:** With so many thousands of kilometres of coastline, Florida has a large variety of ports, marinas and docks. Most major cruise lines regularly dock in a Florida port, and yacht charters are available to and from the region. An abundance of ferry services operate from mainland destinations to the offshore barrier islands.

## What to Pack

Florida, generally, is very casual. Pack according to season. Take a jumper in winter, particularly if visiting the north of the state. In summer, pack light, loose clothing for humid weather and be prepared for tropical rainstorms. You'll need plenty of sun cream and don't forget sunglasses and a hat. Comfortable shoes are a necessity for theme parks, which usually require a lot of walking and queueing. In summer, mosquitoes and other biting bugs are rampant, so take enough repellent. Don't worry if you do forget something; it will be available across the state, probably at less cost than at home.

## Money Matters

**Currency:** The official currency is the dollar, symbolized by the $ sign. One dollar is divided into 100 cents in the following denominations: 5 cents (nickel), 10 cents (dime) and 25 cents (quarter). Avoid carrying large sums in cash with you and ideally use US currency traveller's cheques. Note that cheques in pound sterling and other European currencies will not be changed except at the bigger banks. Major credit cards are widely accepted and most Americans use plastic rather than cash.

**Exchange:** Foreign exchange desks are located at airports and a few large banks and hotels. Banks are generally open

10:00–15:00 Mon–Thu, and 10:00–17:00 Fri.

Hotels and car hire companies may require a credit card swipe before handing over a vehicle or checking you in.

**Tipping:** Most restaurants and bars add a 15% service charge to your bill, but an additional tip is expected for good service. Taxi drivers expect at least 10% in tips, and airport and hotel porters demand a minimum of US$1 per bag.

**Sales tax:** The six per cent is not usually included in the displayed price, and will be added to the bill at the check out point.

## Accommodation

Florida offers an enormous choice of accommodation. Peak season varies from north to south but, generally speaking, if you plan to be in the south in winter or in the north in summer, book ahead. Accommodation varies from inexpensive motels to high-rise tourist hotels. Luxury resorts are often low-rise and spread over hundreds of acres.

City-centre hotels and those near the major airports tend to cater for business travellers and are priced accordingly.

All the major American hotel chains are well represented in the state and will book you into other chain members elsewhere on request.

Note: the rate is usually for the room, not per person.

Most reservations are kept until 17:00 or 18:00, but this can be extended if the hotel is warned in advance of your late arrival. Most establishments will require at least one night's payment in advance, or a tour operator voucher or proof of payment.

Do not commit yourself unnecessarily to half-board or even bed and breakfast – eating out is so cheap, that many hotels quote a simple room rate knowing guests prefer to eat elsewhere.

## Eating Out

Florida prides itself on its fresh seafood and freshly grown fruits and vegetables. Portions are large and prices generally

low. Meals can be true feasts, with pancakes and massive omelettes for breakfast, and eat-as-much-as-you-can buffets in the evening.

On Sunday, breakfast and lunch will often be merged into brunch, a massive banquet, frequently served with a glass of champagne, orange juice or a Bloody Mary.

It is interesting to note the regional differences within the state. To the north the food is influenced by Southern cooking and Creole cuisine. Grits, okra (a long, thin vegetable), fried aubergine (eggplant), fried chicken and corn bread are among the staples. Further south the cooking is influenced by 20th-century immigrants. Spicy Cuban and Caribbean foods are commonplace in Miami, where Spanish style also abounds. Alligator is on the menu seasonally: it tastes a bit like chicken, and is reassuringly eco-friendly, coming from a well-orchestrated culling programme. In the Keys, the food is slightly different again – there is much more delectable seafood and tasty Key lime pie for dessert.

## Transport

**Air:** All major US carriers fly into Florida, while American Eagle, Delta and USAir offer comprehensive networks within Florida. The air passes of some airlines cost much the same as bus or rail tickets – a good bargain.

**Road:** Road networks are good, with major and interstate highways (motorways) running north to south and east to west.

| CONVERSION CHART | | |
|---|---|---|
| **From** | **To** | **Multiply By** |
| Millimetres | Inches | 0.0394 |
| Metres | Yards | 1.0936 |
| Metres | Feet | 3.281 |
| Kilometres | Miles | 0.6214 |
| Kilometres square | Square miles | 0.386 |
| Hectares | Acres | 2.471 |
| Litres | Pints | 1.760 |
| Kilograms | Pounds | 2.205 |
| Tonnes | Tons | 0.984 |
| To convert Celsius to Fahrenheit: x 9 ÷ 5 + 32 | | |

There are a few toll roads. Most towns and cities are laid out on a grid system, many based on numbered streets, which run in one direction only, with avenues or boulevards intersecting at 90-degree angles. All car rental companies have outlets in the major centres and at airports – shop around for the best deal. Fly-drive packages often present the cheapest and easiest way of arranging a car. Anyone over 16, with a valid driving licence, can drive in Florida, though most rental companies insist that drivers be over 25. Insurance may be arranged by the car hire firm.

**Road Rules:** Driving is on the right. Rectangular green road signs usually provide directions, while yellow signs contain safety information. White signs show speed limits: 15mph (24kph) in school zones, 25mph (40kph) on residential streets and between 35–55mph (56–88kph) on main streets. Interstate highways are usually 55mph (90kph) in towns and 65mph (105kph) in rural areas. All front-seat passengers must wear seat belts. Children under three must sit in approved car seats, which rental companies can usually supply. You should drive with headlights on if it rains hard enough to have to use windshield wipers. Florida's anti-drink-drive laws are tough: offenders face heavy fines and possible jail terms. If you park unlawfully or overstay your metered time, your vehicle will be towed away. Parking within three metres of a fire hydrant is an offence. It is illegal to leave animals in parked cars.

**Buses:** Local networks mostly run on routes planned for residents and commuters rather than tourists, and serve cities, counties or beach areas. Check route and times before tackling local services – most require an exact fare. Greyhound operates interstate and serves the major cities. Cities like Miami have buses arriving almost hourly; others only have daily or weekly services, so check ahead and plan carefully.

**Rail:** Railway services are not so good in Florida. Amtrak never offers more than two services a day to any city. Rail passes, bought before leaving home, can cut the cost. Travel agents in Europe sell both Greyhound and Amtrak tickets and can book on specified services.

## Business Hours

Most shopping malls are open 10:00–21:00 Mon–Sat, 10:00–18:00 Sun. Other shops and offices generally open 09:00–17:00 Mon–Sat. Most offices are closed on Saturday.

## Time Difference

Florida has two time zones. Most of the state operates on Eastern Standard Time while the northwest region, west of the Apalachicola River, operates on Central Standard Time. Eastern Standard Time is five hours behind Greenwich Mean (or Universal Standard) Time (GMT) in winter, while Central Standard Time is six hours behind. Florida has United States Daylight Saving Time, advancing clocks by one hour from the last Sunday in April to the last Sunday in October.

### PUBLIC HOLIDAYS

**1 January** • New Year's Day
**15 January** •
Martin Luther King's Birthday
**Third Monday in February** •
Presidents Day
**March** • Good Friday
(half-day holiday)
**March** • Easter Monday
**Last Monday in May** •
Memorial Day
**4 July** • Independence Day
**First Monday in September** •
Labor Day
**Second Monday in October** •
Columbus Day
**11 November** •
Veterans Day
**Last Thursday in November** •
Thanksgiving Day
**25 December** •
Christmas Day
Most Americans have only one day off at Christmas and Easter. Halloween (October 31) is almost a holiday with kids 'trick or treating'.

## Communications

Postal services are generally very efficient. Stamps can be bought (at a small extra cost) from hotels and vending machines or at post offices. Post offices are usually open 09:00–17:00 Mon–Fri, 09:00–12:00 Sat. Post your letters in blue mailboxes on the street, in post offices or hotel lobbies. Mail to Europe takes about one week to arrive.

The international telephone dialling code for the United States is 1.

Most hotels have direct dial telephones for international calls to Europe, although a credit card imprint may be required before you are allowed to use one. Phone cards are the most economical and most hotels have public call boxes. Public telephones can be found on street corners, at bars, restaurants, hotel lobbies, bus and rail stations. An automated voice will ask you to insert coins. The phone may ring immediately after you finish a call to request more money. If you do not comply, the person you called will be billed. Non-local and long-distance calls are cheaper between 18:00 and 08:00. International calls are cheapest between 23:00 and 07:00. Many tourist agencies, theme parks, attractions and car hire firms have a toll-free number (prefix 800 or 888), which can only be accessed free from inside the United States.

## Electricity

The electricity circuit runs on 110 volts, which means that equipment from many European and other countries will not work without an adaptor. The American plugs are two-pronged, but some adaptors don't fit US sockets, so you are advised to check when buying.

## Weights and Measures

All measures are imperial in the US. Petrol is bought in US gallons, which are smaller than the European gallon. Clothing sizes are smaller – buy a US size 10 if you would normally wear a European size 12. For shoes, add one to the measurement (i.e. try on a size five when you would normally wear a size four).

## Health Precautions

Florida is a safe and healthy place. Water is safe to drink and food hygiene standards generally excellent. The sun is strong, so take sun cream, hats and sunglasses to avoid sunburn. If on medication, take sufficient with you – it will be available but may be more costly in Florida.

## Health Services

Health services throughout Florida are comprehensive but expensive. Make sure you are properly insured, including sufficient for repatriation if necessary. Hotels usually have a doctor on call 24 hours a day.

## Personal Safety

As in any major tourist area worldwide, tourists can become targets. A few common-sense guidelines minimize any risk:

• Do not carry large sums of cash or wear a lot of jewellery.
• Do not walk around empty or unlit streets at night.
• Park in well-lit areas only.
• Ask for directions before leaving the hotel or airport.
• If you get lost, find a well-lit petrol station or public building to ask for assistance.
• Some rental companies offer mobile phones for use in emergencies – use them.
• If you are bumped from behind while driving, do not stop. Drive somewhere safe, then call the police if necessary.
• Do not open your door without checking who it is.
• Do not take valuables to the beach with you – keep them in the hotel safe.

• In any emergency call **911**. The police have multilingual staff working on help lines with tourist advice.

## Emergencies

The **police**, **ambulance** and **fire service** can be contacted by dialling **911**.
Companies issuing traveller's cheques may be reached on toll-free numbers in the US. Keep this number separate from your cheques and call immediately if you have lost your cheques or had them stolen. The British Consulate has an office in Miami, tel: (305) 374-1522, which you should contact if you lose your passport. Also, report stolen or lost passports or traveller's cheques to the police.

## Etiquette

Florida is a friendly place with a relaxed ambience. Dress codes are usually equally relaxed – in the evenings, however, you may want to cover up.

| GOOD READING |
| --- |

• Brogan, Hugh (1990) *The Penguin History of the United States of America*. Penguin.
• Bryson, Bill (1996) *Made in America*. Minerva.
• Carr, Archie Fairly (1955) *Guide to the Reptiles, Amphibians and Freshwater Fishes of Florida*. FUP.
• Rawlings, Marjorie Kinnan (1992) *The Yearling*. Mammoth.
• Hemingway, Ernest (1976) *The Old Man and the Sea*. Triad; (1990) *Islands in the Stream*. Grafton.

# INDEX

Note: Numbers in **bold** indicate photographs